THE SHADE OF HOMER

A STUDY IN MODERN GREEK POETRY

DAVID RICKS

LECTURER IN MODERN GREEK STUDIES,
KING'S COLLEGE LONDON

CAMBRIDGE UNIVERSITY PRESS

CAMBRIDGE

NEW YORK PORT CHESTER

MELBOURNE SYDNEY

Published by the Press Syndicate of the University of Cambridge
The Pitt Building, Trumpington Street, Cambridge CB2 1RP
32 East 57th Street, New York, NY 10022, USA
10 Stamford Road, Oakleigh, Melbourne 3166, Australia

First published 1989

Printed in Great Britain by the University Press, Cambridge

British Library cataloguing in publication data

Ricks, David.
The shade of Homer: a study in modern Greek poetry
1. Poetry in modern Greek, to 1980 – Critical studies
I. Title
889′.1′009

Library of Congress cataloguing in publication data

Ricks, David.
The shade of Homer.
Bibliography: p.
Includes index.
1. Greek poetry, Modern–19th century–History and criticism.
2. Greek poetry, Modern–20th century–History and criticism.
3. Homer–Influence. I. Title.
PA5250.R54 1989 889′.1′009 88-35204

ISBN 0 521 36663 1

CONTENTS

ACKNOWLEDGEMENTS

This book could not have been written without the generosity of the British Academy, which awarded the author a Major State Studentship (1982–5) and a Post-Doctoral Research Fellowship (1986–9). Professor R. M. Beaton supervised the doctoral thesis out of which this study has grown, providing valued advice on matters of scope and detail alike; the examiners, Mr C. F. Robinson and Dr M. S. Silk, made further useful comments. The publisher's readers of the typescript did much to establish the form and priorities of the book version; I am also grateful to Dr D. W. Holton and Dr P. A. Mackridge for their careful perusal of the whole typescript. In addition, sections were read at various stages by Dr D. A. Jacob, Dr G. Kehayoglu and my wife, Catherine Ricks.

A version of chapter 5 appeared in *Keats–Shelley Journal*.

PREFACE

> What we want is to disturb and alarm the public; to upset its reliance upon Shakespeare, Nelson, Wellington and Sir Isaac Newton; to point out that at any moment the relation of a modern Englishman to Shakespeare may be discovered to be that of a modern Greek to Aeschylus.
>
> T. S. ELIOT[1]

The Burden of the Past, the Anxiety of Influence: however we term it, the subject of the poet's relation to his predecessors is one that the late twentieth century finds compelling; and the reader of this book will no doubt be hoping to learn something more about this phenomenon. It has after all been acknowledged that 'everyone who now reads and writes in the West, of whatever racial background, sex or ideological camp, is still a son or daughter of Homer'.[2] What is the importance of Homer for the poets of modern Greece? Is he a helper, a kindly ancestral shade who speaks to them across the ages, or a handicap, a shadow that will loom over their efforts for ever?

Eliot's remark above is an important sign that in the poetry of modern Greece there may be something from which the West as a whole can learn. Not that the remark was made in that spirit: it is in the context of a campaign against the complacency of English critics with respect to the place of 'tradition' in English life and letters that Eliot chooses the modern Greek case as uncontroversially incompatible with established notions of tradition as continuity. Mentioning the modern Greek and Aeschylus – chosen above Homer here, it seems, to make a closer parallel with Shakespeare – is to take the modern Englishman down a peg or two. To European eyes the Greek is a Modern Greek – a different animal, that is, from the Ancient Greek – and Eliot means to infect us with the suspicion that, in some sense, the modern Englishman may not be quite an Englishman.

[1] T. S. Eliot, 'Observations', *The Egoist* 5 (1918), 69–70.
[2] Harold Bloom, *A Map of Misreading* (New York 1975), p. 33.

Eliot, then, took the modern Greeks as a debating point: only in the case of Mr Eugenides did he bother to be disparaging. And it has only been since 1918, when Eliot's remark was made, that the poetry of modern Greece has become internationally known, largely through the work of Cavafy and Seferis. It is these two poets, together with Angelos Sikelianos, a contemporary little known outside Greece and too little read within it, that are the principal subject of this study. It is thanks in large measure to this triumvirate – each member of which had his origins outside the capital in Athens – that we can properly speak of Modern Greek Poetry rather than of poetry in Modern Greek; of a part of European, as opposed to a manifestation of Balkan, literature. In particular, these three poets, each from a different starting-point and each in a very different manner, succeed in the high national aspiration of finding Homer some role in the modern poetry; and they do so in a group of poems composed in the duration of a single poet's working lifetime (1892–1940).

This, in brief, is the achievement discussed in this book, one facet of a broader achievement which has not gone unacknowledged: 'The Greek War of Independence broke out in 1821. Since that date, the vitality of Greece has manifested itself in many ways. But perhaps nothing has been so striking as the growth and fecundity of her intellectual life. And here pride of place goes to the poets and to poetry.' But it is a sobering thought that this passage, which was written in 1955, prefaced the last general book published in England on modern Greek poetry, Philip Sherrard's *The Marble Threshing Floor*; a book, indeed, which was concerned, in the author's words, 'with the ideas of the poetry rather than with questions of style or biography, source or influence'.[3] These latter problems are of course especially inaccessible to the foreign reader. In 1940 Romilly Jenkins began his book on Solomos with the words: 'It is an ironical fact that there should be in this country today hardly more than a dozen persons familiar with the name of Dionysius Solomos; ironical because the exclusive nationalism which invaded European life and thought in the nineteenth century was very largely the outcome

[3] Philip Sherrard, *The Marble Threshing Floor* (London 1956), p.v.

of that Romantic movement of which Solomos himself was so characteristic a representative.'[4] Given the problem of the accessibility of modern Greek poetry, it is perhaps worth my setting out here how this book sees its audience.

This book assumes a willingness to approach modern Greek poetry at close quarters. But I have tried to keep in mind, throughout, the reader of modern European poetry who may be little acquainted with the poetry of Greece but who is nonetheless interested in the problem which is explored in these pages and its relation to poetry with which he is more familiar. To aid the exposition, accordingly, all the relevant poems are quoted in their entirety in translations of my own; these have no pretensions to literary merit. (Certain indispensable references to the original Greek will be made in discussion.) I have felt it reasonable to presume that the non-specialist reader will be interested rather in modern Greek poems than in modern Greek literary history; I have, however, compiled a reading list of items in English which should provide novices with their bearings; in addition, I have given dates of birth and publication in the text throughout, which should help the reader who will turn to a work of reference. (The reader should be aware that in transliterating modern Greek proper names I normally follow the system of the *Journal of Modern Greek Studies*, with the difference that stress marks are included on the name's first appearance only.) Although the core of this book consists of a series of close, even strenuous readings, its author has attempted to bear in mind throughout the aspiration eloquently stated by Henry Gifford:

> Eliot cannot be challenged when he says that poetry has 'a unique value for the people of the poet's race and language, which it can have for no other'. Yet it becomes possible for practised readers of poetry to hear in a foreign poem ... a specific national tone which they too begin to appreciate, and thereby to enlarge their sympathies, even their capacity for feeling.[5]

[4] Romilly Jenkins, *Dionysius Solomós* (Cambridge 1940), p. 1.

[5] Henry Gifford, *Poetry in a Divided World* (Cambridge 1986), pp. 85–6.

I should also say a word about this book's envisaged specialist audience, and in the first instance the undergraduate studying modern Greek. It is hoped that the theme will be of general interest, especially to those with some classical background; but the book can readily be used selectively: most of these poems are on undergraduate syllabuses but there are not discussions available in English for all of them. (It is assumed that the book will be used in conjunction with the original Greek texts.) As for this book's position as regards the scholar, its subtitle, *A Study in Modern Greek Poetry*, is intended to indicate its modest ambitions: it is rather an extended essay on an idea and its implications for poetic practice than in any sense a work of reference. Notes have been deliberately kept to a minimum, and the author confesses to having been haunted by the words of E. R. Dodds: 'If the love and knowledge of Greek literature ever die in this country, they will die of a suffocation arising from its exponents' industry. I do not wish to be accessory to the murder.'[6] The reader seeking some of the less readily available Greek texts and certain further details is advised to turn to the doctoral thesis in which this book originates.[7]

Beyond these points of presentation, however, there is one of scope. Despite the generality of this book's title, I have felt it important, on the one hand, to concentrate solely on works which have some direct connection with the *Iliad* and the *Odyssey* – as opposed to works which make vaguer thematic or mythological reference – and, on the other, to limit myself to a small selection of poems. Anyone who knows much about modern Greek poetry will see that I have omitted some well-known poems, poems which for my purposes – the furthering of the central discussion – I felt to be neither interestingly successful nor interestingly failed. In gathering the material for this book I found the vagueness and superficiality which characterized too many existing treatments to be partly the result of the very wealth of material that could be regarded as relevant; and to admit that the choice of poems discussed in this book is neither complete nor indisputably representative is to

[6] E. R. Dodds (ed.), Euripides, *Bacchae* (2nd edition, Oxford 1960), p. vi.

[7] D. B. Ricks, 'Homer and Greek Poetry 1888–1940: Cavafy, Sikelianos, Seferis' (Ph.D., London 1986).

affirm that the relation of the modern Greek poets to Homer can be only qualitatively, and not quantitatively, assessed. This book is founded on the priorities laid down by Randall Jarrell:

> Nothing would have more value for criticism than the existence of a few hundred or thousand detailed critical analyses ... of important English poems ... *important* includes good and bad.[8]

A preoccupation with poems in their individuality, and with their relations as individuals, was given memorable expression by a great writer of the short poem, Robert Frost:

> A poem is best read in the light of all the other poems ever written. We read *A* the better to read *B* (we have to start somewhere, we may get very little out of *A*). We read *B* the better to read *C*, *C* the better to read *D*, *D* the better to go back and get something more out of *A*. Progress is not the aim but circulation. The thing is to get among the poems where they hold each other apart in their places as the stars do.[9]

In the case of the Greek poets and Homer, however, we shall have to bear in mind a crucial adjustment of Frost's comparison that is made by an epigrammatist of unknown date, Leonidas of Tarentum (*Anthologia Palatina* 9.24):

> The Sun, driving his fiery chariot,
> darkens the stars and the holy cycles of the Moon;
> Homer has cast into obscurity the poets in a herd,
> holding up the Muses' brightest light.

This is the problem that we shall be examining in the Introduction.

[8] Randall Jarrell, *Kipling, Auden and Company* (New York 1980), p. 64.

[9] In Reuben A. Brower, *The Poetry of Robert Frost. Constellations of Intention* (Oxford 1963), p. vii.

Introduction: Homer and the modern Greek poets

I

> The greatest fact remains always the precociously panhellenic HOMER. All good things derive from him; yet at the same time he remained the mightiest obstacle of all. He made everyone else superficial, and this is why the really serious spirits struggled against him. But to no avail. Homer always won.[1]

Nietzsche's statement here about the relation of the classical Greeks to Homer is characteristically thought-provoking. But it clearly describes a relation which differs from that we shall expect to find in the case of the modern Greeks. Searching for parallels rather among the English moderns, the contemporaries of the Greek poets who are the subject of this book, two cases spring to mind – that is, if we discount Homer himself, whose influence on English poetry, as opposed to English letters, has been somewhat marginal.[2] The most obvious example of a parallel is that of Shakespeare, but Dante too has exerted a significant influence on English poets in the last two centuries.[3] Now in modern Greece lip-service is certainly paid to the central place of Homer in the culture; and yet Homer in Greece lacks the cultural pervasiveness of Shakespeare in England. This is partly a matter of form – the theatre-going public is larger than the serious reading public – and partly a matter of language. Primrose path; hoist with his own petard; a palpable hit; caviare to the general; dog will have his day – these phrases from just one play by Shakespeare belong to everyone, including those unaware of their provenance. In Greece, by contrast, although anyone who has

[1] Friedrich Nietzsche, 'Notes for "We Philologists"', tr. William Arrowsmith, *Arion* (n.s.) 1 (1973), 279–380; quotation from p. 335.

[2] Useful and contrasting treatments in Richard Jenkyns, *The Victorians and Ancient Greece* (Oxford 1980) and Frank M. Turner, *The Greek Heritage in Victorian Britain* (New Haven 1981).

[3] See Jonathan Bate, *Shakespeare and the English Romantic Imagination* (Oxford 1986); Steve Ellis, *Dante and English Poetry. Shelley to T. S. Eliot* (Cambridge 1983) and Stuart Y. McDougal (ed.), *Dante Among the Moderns* (Chapel Hill and London 1985).

been to school can spout the first line of the *Odyssey*, the number of Homeric phrases which are genuinely current can be counted on the fingers of one hand: αἰὲν ἀριστεύειν ('always to excel'), εἷς οἰωνὸς ἄριστος ('one omen is best [to fight for one's homeland]') and the hideous misquotation ζείδωρος αὖρα ('life-giving breeze', for ἄρουρα, 'ground'). Despite this, the modern Greeks, not surprisingly, look on Homer as an ancestor, while Dante, say, is only metaphorically seen as an ancestor by the English poet. The achievement of the poets of independent Greece in making themselves, as poets, the descendants of Homer – well aware that they cannot struggle against him – raises distinctive issues without exact parallel which deserve a sustained treatment.

Surprisingly, however, there has only been one real attempt to provide one. In the wake of Seferis' collected poems of 1946, the critic Dimítris Nikolareïzis published a brief but stimulating essay, 'The Presence of Homer in Modern Greek Poetry', which remains fundamental for the exploration of the subject.[4] Its particular value lies in its recognition of the fact that Homeric allusion in modern Greek poetry is not a self-explanatory feature of technique: most importantly, Nikolareïzis suggested that the Asia Minor Disaster of 1922, through which more than a million Greeks suffered an enforced return from Asia Minor to Greece proper – abandoning Smyrna, the city most proverbially associated with Homer – was a crucial dividing-line in modern Greece's consciousness of its ancestor. And in general Nikolareïzis' essay goes some way, in its own terms, to meeting a demand for a study of the modern Greek poet as heir.[5]

Yet there are important differences – apart, obviously, from that of scale – between Nikolareïzis' discussion and my own. It is true that his treatment of five poets together – Solomós (1798–1857), Sikelianós (1884–1951), Kazantzakis (1883–1957), Seferis (1900–1971) and Elytis (b. 1911) – is a valuable model, prompting as it does thoughts not just about each poet's relation to Homer, but

[4] Dimítris Nikolareîzis, «Ἡ παρουσία τοῦ Ὁμήρου στὴ νέα ἐλληνικὴ ποίηση», Νέα Ἑστία no. 491 (Christmas 1947), 153–64.

[5] See Christopher Ricks, 'Allusion: the Poet as Heir', *Studies in the Eighteenth Century* 3 (ed. R. F. Brissenden and J. C. Eade, Canberra 1976), 209–40.

also – a subject on which these poets are not surprisingly more reticent – about their relation to one another. While never stating the point that the two relations are necessarily intertwined, Nikolareïzis laid the ground for the point to be developed; here, however, the point is developed in rather a different way.

In the first place, the choice of poets here is not the same. This book, as I have indicated in the Preface, is a study of just one phase in the poetry of modern Greece; and the beginning of the Second World War for Greece in 1940 has been taken, not too arbitrarily, as the end of that phase. (The post-war period deserves a separate study; a few observations appear at the end of this book.) At the other end chronologically, the national poet, Solomos, figures rather as part of the prehistory of the phase under discussion; I have, furthermore, felt it important to include with him the rival poetic programme of Andréas Kálvos (1792–1869) and some material on the neglected years between Solomos and Kostís Palamás (1859–1943). With reference to Palamas himself, it was evidently felt by Nikolareïzis that Palamas' poems on Homeric themes were not among his best – they are not – and that they occupied a peripheral position in his *œuvre*. But Palamas deserves some attention nonetheless.

There remains one important omission from my account and one from Nikolareïzis'. The former is the *Odyssey* of Nikos Kazantzakis; the reason is one of genre.[6] The creation of a new epic – and a 33,333-line one at that – in a new epic metre (the seventeen-syllable line) and idiom (demoticism at its lexical extreme) is an utterly different enterprise from the writing of a short poem alluding to the ancient epic. Kazantzakis' choice of title, especially in the iconoclastic spelling 'Οδύσεια, indicates a grand gesture of ambition, as does his creation of myriad compound epithets to rival Homer's: the project and its implementation are quite different from those discussed in this book. The startling omission from Nikolareïzis' account, on the other hand, is Cavafy (1863–1933). Nikolareïzis, it seems, saw Cavafy's physical absence from Greece proper – he visited Greece only twice in his life – as denying him

[6] Nikos Kazantzakis, 'Οδύσεια (Athens 1938).

access to Homeric inspiration. My treatment of the relevant poems of Cavafy, by contrast, seeks to face the problem by looking at the sources of his inspiration primarily in poetry – poetry in English, at that – and by seeing how successfully such material is, as it were, naturalized in Greek. (Because these poems by Cavafy lead on less directly from his Greek predecessors than does the work of Sikelianos I have placed the chapter on the older poet second in defiance of chronology.)

This takes us on to a more general and more significant difference of outlook, concerning the interpretation of tradition. Despite his attention to historical context, Nikolareïzis is still haunted by the metaphor of *presence* that we find in his title; so what he writes by way of conclusion is this: 'Homer's poetry is present in the contemporary Greek poetic consciousness' – and the Greek word for presence is, significantly, *parousia*. One cannot escape the feeling that Homer is seen as a Messiah arrived in his Kingdom rather than as one invited there by the craft and dedication of the later poets. And Nikolareïzis' view of the Greek tradition – a highly representative one – is in tune with the metaphor of presence. He writes of the relation between the modern Greek poet and his oldest ancestor as follows:

> It is in these three sources of Hellenism, language, the spirit of the folk and nature, that the imagination of each of the poets mentioned dipped its wings; and out of the most genuine Hellenic elements each of them moulded his poetic visions according to his temperament.[7]

Now a Hellenic national consciousness going back much beyond 1821 is an easy target for the sceptic; nor is the natural world as a criterion for a poetic tradition any more satisfactory, for it would exclude the Alexandrian Cavafy. A poem is made of words, and it is with the 'first source' of language that any study of modern Greek poetry and tradition must begin. For although the debate about what is or is not 'genuinely Greek' in the Greek language is one that

[7] Nikolareïzis, «Παρουσία», p. 154.

will never end, there *is* a Greek language, as a distinguished Western authority affirms:

> It cannot be too much emphasized that Greek is one language, and not a series of distinct languages. If one wants to learn Greek, it does not really matter whether one begins with Homer, with Plato, with the New Testament, with the Romance of Digenis Akritas, or with Kazantzakis... And educated Greek speakers have always had present in their minds the whole of the language up to their own time, drawn upon it, alluded to it, and consciously modified it.[8]

It is this question of language that must ultimately distinguish the Greek poet from his Western counterpart when he alludes to Homer, even if that counterpart, like the Sicilian Salvatore Quasimodo, hails Mycenae as a citizen of the ancient Greek world.[9] But it is precisely this question of language that has barely been addressed by critics. In Nikolareïzis' case, the omission is not surprising: he is thinking, in Romantic terms, of poets rather than poems, and of the authenticity of their inspiration rather than of their way with words; and yet without reference to the language issue in relation to specific poems we shall be left with unhelpful generalizations about the 'continuity' of the Greek language. And while the question has been especially neglected with respect to Greek poetry in the modern period, it arises with respect to all Greek poetry after Homer:

> When, in a poem in which every word tells (in Sappho, for example) we come across what I have called a 'dead expression', an ornamental epithet borrowed from Homer, should we be shocked or delighted? Is it simply a cliché and therefore a defect in the poem, or is it a conscious archaism, a judicious borrowing from an honoured tradition?
>
> Despite the interest of scholars in the survival of Homeric language into later literature I am not aware that the sharp aesthetic problem raised by this survival has been properly examined.[10]

[8] Robert Browning, *Medieval and Modern Greek* (2nd edition, Cambridge 1983), pp. vii–viii.

[9] Salvatore Quasimodo, 'Mycenae', in *Selected Writings* (tr. Allen Mandelbaum, New York 1960), pp. 230–1.

[10] A. E. Harvey, 'Homeric Epithets in Greek Lyric Poetry', *Classical Quarterly* (n.s.) 7 (1957), 206–23; quotation from p. 207.

The Greek language may be one, but it has not of course remained the same; and we should not assume that the problem as stated above has remained the same, although it does indeed remain. Before we return to look at it in detail, we should consider in more general terms the complex fate of the modern Greek poet. If we reject as inadequate the notion that Homer is simply *present* in tradition, what view of that tradition are we to put in its place? What is the relation that prevails between the modern Greek poet and his greatest ancestor?

II

In recent years two well-known manifestoes, by Walter Jackson Bate and Harold Bloom respectively, have demanded that critics accord a higher priority to the study of poetic influence.[11] The problem is stated most epigrammatically in some words quoted by Bate which were written by an Egyptian scribe of 2000 B.C.:

> Would I had phrases that are not known, utterances that are strange, in new language that has not been used, free from repetition, not an utterance which has grown stale, which men of old have spoken.[12]

Each of these influential books discussing the problem, it is no disparagement to say, is in the nature of an extrapolation from Eliot's magisterial essay of 1944, 'What is a Classic?' (though it says volumes about the importance of the question of influence that Eliot is not acknowledged by both of his successors with equal generosity). I quote from the core of this:

> Just as we sometimes observe men whose lives are overshadowed by the fame of a father or a grandfather, men of whom any achievement of which they are capable appears comparatively insignificant, so a late age of poetry may be consciously impotent to compete with its distinguished ancestry.[13]

[11] Walter Jackson Bate, *The Burden of the Past and the English Poet* (London 1970); Harold Bloom, *The Anxiety of Influence* (New York 1973).

[12] Bate, *Burden*, pp. 3–4.

[13] T. S. Eliot, *Of Poetry and Poets* (London 1979), pp. 57–8.

Here is the model developed by both Bate and Bloom; but it is important to note that Eliot is here speaking, not of poets, but of ages. Bate and Bloom are themselves concerned with distinct ages – from the Renaissance to the present (and in particular with the years 1660–1830) in the former case and from the Enlightenment to the present in the latter – but Eliot raises the possibility of a new relation to an earlier age altogether, one which would be, in Dryden's much-quoted phrase, 'the Gyant Race before the Flood'.[14] With respect to the poetry of modern Greece this phrase has a resonance even greater than that which it possesses with respect to Dryden's (and Bate's) Flood, the Restoration or to Bloom's Enlightenment, after which 'the question of influence became central to poetic consciousness'.[15] For it seems, on the face of it, that the poetry of modern Greece – of Greece since 1821 – is forever divided from ancient Greek poetry by one or both of two dates. The first is 146 B.C., when Rome conquered Greece, and, to quote Dryden once again, 'with *Grecian* Spoils brought *Grecian* Numbers home'; the second is 1453, when Constantinople, 'the City' to the Greeks, was captured by the Ottomans.[16] Of course, Bate and Bloom alike acknowledge that the problem of influence varies in its acuteness according to time and place; but in the modern Greek case we have circumstances which demand special attention, even if our ultimate goal is still 'to foster a more adequate practical criticism'.[17]

It was a classical scholar of distinction who was himself a Greek, Johannes Sykutris (1901–37), who most unashamedly and unequivocally acknowledged the newness of modern Hellenism. He began an essay of 1928 by reiterating the essential fact that the word 'Hellene' had long been reserved in Greek parlance for the pagans;

[14] John Dryden, 'To My Dear Friend Mr Congreve', *Poems* (ed. James Kinsley, Oxford 1970), p. 852; see, e.g., Bate, *Burden*, pp. 26–7 and Bloom, *Anxiety*, p. 11.

[15] Bloom, *Anxiety*, p. 11; the author has since recanted this view (*A Map of Misreading*, p. 77).

[16] Dryden, 'To the Earl of Roscomon', *Poems*, p. 387; see in this connection two poems of Cavafy: (on 146 B.C.) «Εἰς Ἰταλικὴν παραλίαν», Ποιήματα (ed. G. P. Savidis, Athens 1981) vol. 2, p. 46 and (on A.D. 1453) «Πάρθεν», Ἀνέκδοτα ποιήματα (1882–1923) (ed. G. P. Savidis 1968), pp. 183–5.

[17] Variations in the problem of influence: Bate, *Burden*, pp. 3–4; Bloom, *Anxiety*, p. 68; quotation from Bloom, *Anxiety*, p. 5.

and he went on to examine the revival of the term in the War of Independence:

> On the one hand the ideal of ancient Greece was the common bond which united and gave support to the Nation's forces and forged them for the stern struggle; on the other, it banished all those elements which Byzantine tradition or ecclesiastical internationalism had gathered into one. From out of the chaos of the Christian nationalities of the East it separated and made whole the Greek nationality *as a nationality*; out of the *Roman* (Ρωμαῖος) it created the *Hellene*. This is the deeper significance possessed by the bringing back of our national appellation... Whoever persists in considering it to be a blind and temporary romanticism provokes the harshest indictment of his ability to understand or judge of the facts of history.
>
> And so the '21 genuinely constitutes a break with the past and 'tradition'; but the tradition being that of the Byzantine period and of Greece under Turkish rule. At the same time, however, it constitutes a renascence, a renascence of the Hellenic spirit (as the people of the time were able to comprehend it), a conscious return to the deeds of the ancestors and – through the Romantic's bold leap over the Roman and Byzantine periods – a direct continuation of those deeds. The names of Leonidas and Themistocles adorn not just the prows that belong to the seamen of Hydra – they constitute living presences, they stand by those in struggle, they become models and ideas which shape the sensibilities and energies of the descendants. The nation feels that it is a *nation*; it feels its rights as the heir of past greatness and its duties towards it.

But, as Sykutris went on to observe, the early attempts to build on this sense of Hellenic identity in any educational or literary terms were largely unsuccessful: 'Of Homer they learned only the story of the Trojan War, lots and lots of vocabulary, a few elements of metrics... without attaining the level of a basic sense of the rhythm.'[18] And this was largely true of the poetry of the new Hellas.

[18] Ioánnis Sikutrís, «Ἐπιλεγόμενα εἰς τὸ ἔργον τοῦ Th. Zielinski Ἡμεῖς καὶ οἱ ἀρχαῖοι», in Μελέται καὶ ἄρθρα (Athens 1956), pp. 93–119; quotations from pp. 100–2 and 105.

In the history of poetry in Greek the period from 1821 to the present is indeed a classic age; but the achievement has not been brought about without struggle. The modern Greek poets labour under the disadvantage that they are not only modern, with the anxieties that that may imply, but also Greeks; not only Greeks but Modern. The term *Modern Greek* is itself revealing; for in 1821, at the very birth of the new Hellas, one of its foremost creators, culturally if not militarily, was already speaking of it as poetically belated. Byron's 'Isles of Greece', that is, is followed in its context in *Don Juan* by the lines (canto 3 stanza 87),

> Thus sung or would or could or should have sung
> The modern Greek in tolerable verse.
> If not like Orpheus quite, when Greece was young,
> Yet in these times he might have done much worse.

On the one hand the word 'modern' tends to mark off the modern Greek as not being quite Greek; on the other the word 'Greek' inevitably ties him to a distant past with which unflattering comparisons are all too easily made. The consequence is that the modern Greek poet's relation to his ancestors is especially problematic: in choosing the ancestors with whom he, as a poet, can live, he cannot simply 'leapfrog' the parental generation. He must attempt to bridge the Flood that lies between him and ancient Hellenism; and this means overcoming central doubts about his own cultural identity.[19] The ancient Greeks, politically disunited though they were, were unequivocally Hellenes; the modern Greeks, despite the existence of a Greek nation-state, have been engaged in a struggle to live up to their newly readopted appellation 'Hellene'. They have renounced once for all their Byzantine identity as 'Romans' (though the term ρωμιός does survive as an informal racial term of self-identification) and they have become Hellenes. (There is a marked contrast here with the folk culture of the years of Ottoman rule, in which the Hellenes were seen as an extinct super-race of often literally prediluvian giants.) Of course, to acknowledge that the Neohellenic identity is to a large degree the product of the En-

[19] For the notion of 'leapfrogging' see Bate, *Burden*, p. 22; developed by C. Ricks, 'Allusion'.

lightenment is not to concede that modern Greece really owes all that it is to the West or that the modern Greek poet's relation to Homer is a bogus one. J. Th. Kakridis has stated the point as follows:

> the contacts of the modern Greek people with the ancient Hellenes, however one-sided they may have been, and however weirdly they came about, are neither lacking in fascination nor without historical importance. It was incumbent on the new Greek generations to hallow the image of Hellas that was recaptured during the War of Liberation and to make its contact with the Hellenic world more fruitful.[20]

This view, evidently, assumes that living up to the ancient Hellenic ideal was a desirable goal. But it is important to recognize that from a thorough-going Orthodox perspective the change in the Greek was malign:

> Until 1821 we had no problem in dealing with our ancient heritage... through centuries of perseverance, wisdom and sanity, we had managed to cross over from the Hellenic to the Christian form of tradition... It was only after 1821, or perhaps a little earlier, that there appeared here cases of pathological nostalgia for the glory of ancient Greece.[21]

At all events the newness and precariousness of modern Hellenism cannot be over-emphasized.

The modern Greek poet, then, is as modern as any Modern; but he can never remove from his thoughts about the ancients the fact that he is a speaker of Greek; and he thus falls prey not just to modern but to ancient anxieties about Homer: Aeschylus calls his plays 'slices from Homer's great banquets', and Theocritus knows of those who say, 'Homer is enough for all'. The author of the treatise *On the Sublime* discusses the problem of Homer's influence in some detail:

> Plato, if we read him with attention, illustrates another road to sublimity, besides those we have discussed. This is the way

[20] J. Th. Kakridis, 'The Ancient Greeks and the Greeks of the War of Independence', *Balkan Studies* 4 (1963), 251–64; quotation from p. 263.

[21] Zissimos Lorenzatos, *The Lost Center* (tr. Kay Cicelli, Princeton 1980), pp. 130–1.

> of imitation and emulation of great writers of the past... the genius of the ancients acts as a kind of oracular cavern, and effluences flow from it into the minds of their imitators. Even those not previously inclined to prophesy become inspired and share the enthusiasm which comes from the greatness of others. Was Herodotus the only 'most Homeric' writer? Surely Stesichorus and Archilochus earned the name before him. So, more than any, did Plato, who diverted to himself countless rills from the Homeric spring... Plato could not have put such a brilliant finish on his philosophical doctrines or so often risen to poetical subjects and poetical language, if he had not tried, and tried wholeheartedly, to compete for the prize against Homer, like a young aspirant challenging an admired master. To break a lance in this way may well have been a brash and contentious thing to do, but the competition proved anything but valueless. As Hesiod says, 'this strife is good for men'. Truly it is a noble contest and prize of honour, and one well worth winning, in which to be defeated by one's elders is no disgrace.[22]

From this passage we certainly see the centrality of Homer for the Greek author, but the consequences are admittedly unclear: imitation and emulation are two different things, and Longinus, it seems, moves from the former to the latter without quite drawing a distinction between the two.[23] The question of interpretation is important because modern critics, in the wish to bring out the big guns every time, have an inclination to take emulation as subsuming imitation. D. N. Maronítis, for example – the most acute of Greek critics to have devoted attention to the problem of Homeric allusion – has this to say about Alcaeus 42, a sixteen-line lyric which treats of mythical material dealt with in a different way in the *Iliad*: 'And so lyric poetry, through a strictly mythological poem, takes its revenge on heroic poetry. A poetic contest, then, between the epic and lyric worlds in the interior of a mythological poem, with a clear victory for archaic lyric.'[24] But these are reckless words. For ancient lyric

[22] Longinus, 'On the Sublime' 13.2–4; translation quoted from D. A. Russell and M. Winterbottom (eds.), *Ancient Literary Criticism* (Oxford 1972), pp. 475–6.

[23] Discussion in D. A. Russell (ed.), Longinus, *On the Sublime* (Oxford 1964), *ad loc.*

[24] D. N. Maronítis, « Ὁ ἡρωικὸς μῦθος καὶ ἡ λυρικὴ ἀνασκευή του », Διαβάζω no. 107 (1984), 20–6.

poetry, it seems to me, characteristically stakes a claim to nothing more than its own perpetuation in the face of the epic: while drawing extensively on the memory of Homer, that is, it does not attempt to obliterate it or to pit itself against Homer in the manner of the legendary Contest of Homer and Hesiod. A recognition of generic differences will save us from seeing the relation between short lyric poems and epic precursor as an *agon* in which total victory is achievable or even desirable. And this is of course even more tellingly true of the poems produced in a *modern Greece* in which poets are typically more anxious, as we shall see, to establish connections with the oldest poet than to set about challenging him. In modern Greece – with the gigantic exception of Kazantzakis' *Odyssey* – it is imitation rather than emulation of Homer that is the goal.

III

At this point we may return to the question of language. Longinus clearly takes for granted the degree of linguistic continuity which enabled writers like Herodotus and Plato to quote Homeric expressions and phrases with ease; and this is clearly a resource which the modern Greek poet possesses *in some degree* – perhaps to the envy of the poet who writes in another language. But there is a famous statement by Eliot in 'What is a Classic?' that may make the foreign poet grateful that he is not Greek: 'Not only every great poet, but every genuine, though lesser poet, fulfils once for all some possibility of the language, and so leaves one possibility less for his successors.'[25] Homer in particular is not only a great poet but one with a compendiously large vocabulary; a poet, then, all too likely to overshadow the modern Greek poets' attempts to forge powers of expression truly their own. To adapt what Eliot writes in an earlier essay, Homer is certainly remote in time, and to some extent different in interest, from the modern Greek poet; but he is not incontrovertibly alien in language.[26]

But how close is Homer's language to that of the Greek poets of the nineteenth and twentieth centuries A.D.? Perhaps the distance

[25] Eliot, *On Poetry and Poets*, pp. 64–5.

[26] T. S. Eliot, *The Sacred Wood* (London 1977), p. 125.

between the two is such that the modern Greek poet need not really stand in awe at the possibilities of language already fulfilled, because he is using what is essentially a different language. Or to put it another way, perhaps the opportunities which the foreign poet sees as available for the Greek may not really be there. The assessment of linguistic continuity and its relevance to the writer in practice is not easy to establish and does not admit of a simple answer. With reference to Homer's immediate successors, the archaic elegists, the question 'how these poets... use, learn from, reject, and define themselves against the Homeric poems' has long been of interest.[27] But the aesthetic significance of the presence of 'Homeric diction' is not immediately clear:

> We can readily establish which words used by Archilochus occur also in the *Iliad*, *Odyssey* and *Homeric Hymns* and are in that sense 'Homeric'. But if individual words are to be 'Homeric' in an aesthetically significant sense, more is needed: the words must belong solely to the Homeric poems, for only so will their use impart the 'flavour' of Homer.[28]

Similar considerations apply to modern Greek poetry and its relation to Homer. In the least allusive, most colloquial poem of today one can identify a good many nouns, especially, which have remained identical in form and meaning, if not always in associations, since the time of Homer. This, however, does not amount to a Homeric colouring; we may take as a counter-example Louis MacNeice's well-known poem 'Thalassa'.[29] In that poem the title, though comprehensible to one of that poet's background, is intrinsically rich in associations; the Greek poet, by contrast, cannot simply deploy the word θάλασσα and expect his more discerning readers to be impressed or expectant: to this day this word is just the ordinary one used for the sea. That such natural survivals of 'Homeric' language are in fact quite numerous can be illustrated by a look at one of the most quoted poems of the century, 'Préveza' (strictly, 'Province') by Kóstas Kariotákis (1896–1928). The

[27] A. W. H. Adkins, *Poetic Craft in the Early Greek Elegists* (Chicago 1985), p. 22.
[28] Adkins, *Poetic Craft*, p. 34.
[29] Louis MacNeice, *Collected Poems* (London 1979), p. 546.

reason for choosing it is that this is a poet who shocked his readers by employing everyday language and who studiously avoided mythical reference.

ΠΡΕΒΕΖΑ

Θάνατος εἶναι οἱ κάργες ποὺ χτυπιοῦνται
στοὺς μαύρους τοίχους καὶ στὰ κεραμίδια,
θάνατος οἱ γυναῖκες ποὺ ἀγαπιοῦνται
καθὼς νὰ καθαρίζουνε κρεμμύδια.

Θάνατος οἱ λεροί, ἀσήμαντοι δρόμοι,
μὲ τὰ λαμπρά, μεγάλα ὀνόματά τους,
ὁ ἐλαιῶνας, γύρω ἡ θάλασσα, κι ἀκόμη
ὁ ἥλιος, θάνατος μέσα στοὺς θανάτους.

Θάνατος ὁ ἀστυνόμος ποὺ διπλώνει,
γιὰ νὰ ζυγίσει, μιὰ «ἐλλιπῆ» μερίδα,
θάνατος τὰ ζουμπούλια στὸ μπαλκόνι
κι ὁ δάσκαλος μὲ τὴν ἐφημερίδα.

Βάσις, Φρουρά, Ἑξηκονταρχία Πρεβέζης.
Τὴν Κυριακὴ θ' ἀκούσουμε τὴ μπάντα.
Ἐπῆρα ἕνα βιβλιάριο Τραπέζης,
Πρώτη κατάθεσις δραχμαὶ τριάντα.

Περπατῶντας ἀργὰ στὴν προκυμαία,
«ὑπάρχω;» λές, κι ὕστερα «δὲν ὑπάρχεις!»
Φτάνει τὸ πλοῖο. Ὑψωμένη σημαία.
Ἴσως ἔρχεται ὁ κύριος Νομάρχης.

Ἂν τουλάχιστον, μέσα στοὺς ἀνθρώπους
αὐτούς, ἕνας ἐπέθαινε ἀπὸ ἀηδία...
Σιωπηλοί, θλιμμένοι, μὲ σεμνοὺς τρόπους,
θὰ διασκεδάζαμε ὅλοι στὴν κηδεία.

(*Death the crows that beat upon the black walls and the tiles, death the women who make love as if peeling onions. Death the dirty, insignificant streets with their great and glorious names; the olive groves; the sea round about; and the sun, death of deaths. Death the policeman who wraps in paper a 'short-weight' portion in order to weigh it; death the hyacinths on the balcony and the schoolmaster with his paper. Base, Garrison, Preveza Unit. On Sunday we shall hear the band. I got a bank book; first deposit thirty drachmas. Walking slowly on the promenade you say, 'Do I exist?' and then 'You don't!' The boat is coming in. Raised flag. Perhaps it is the Prefect on his way. If, at least, out of all these people, one would die of disgust... Silent, grieved, reverent in manner, we would all have a high time at the funeral.*)[30]

Even this Greek Laforguian uses words that can actually be found in identical forms in the Homeric poems (the words underlined), and these do not include fairly obvious cognates and derivations (the words with spaced-out letters). So many of the words are connectable, by one with a sense of etymology, to the language of Homer that we can speak, with caution, of the modern Greek poet's using the same language.

The language of Homer, it is true, does not permeate that of the moderns as it permeates the post-Homeric poets of the seventh and sixth centuries B.C., Archilochus, Mimnermus, Stesichorus: a crude but revealing test is to try to make out any of the poems discussed in this book with the aid of a Homeric lexicon alone. The continuity of Greek is indeed of unlimited *depth* – right back to Homer; and the modern Greek vocabulary can be of assistance to Homeric exegesis – but it is of limited *breadth*.[31] (Above all, any survivals of Homeric vocabulary occur in a language whose phonology and syntax have undergone wholesale change.) The sense of Homer's dominance over the poetic language is in fact largely a vaguer sense of there being a sort of shadow over the modern poet's words. When Elytis writes,

> The language they gave me Greek;
> poor the house on Homer's shores.
> My sole care my language on Homer's shores.

we can see that Homer's language is still *a* standard, however limited its influence on standard usage.[32] This impression of Homer's dom-

30 K. G. Kariotákis, Ποιήματα καὶ πεζά (ed. G. P. Savidis, Athens 1972), pp. 141–2.
31 See G. P. Shipp, *Modern Greek Evidence for the Ancient Greek Vocabulary* (Sydney 1979).
32 O. Elytis, Τὸ Ἄξιον Ἐστί (Athens 1973), p. 28.

inance right up to the present day is reinforced by the fact that a book in modern Greek is still normally fitted out with the same orthography as the ancient texts. Admittedly, this appearance on the page is to some extent misleading, as it disguises wholesale changes in pronunciation – Chaucer's English, by contrast, *looks* rather more remote than it is – but it is of great psychological importance.

IV

By way of recapitulation, let me state the salient points about the complex relation that prevails between the modern Greek poet and Homer. It is not, in the first place, that which we find in the case of the ancient poets. They are unquestionably Hellenes: the modern Greek poets, by contrast, are engaged in an attempt – which may, like many nationalist projects all over Europe, end in failure – to live up to their new identity as Hellenes. Nor is the relation that of Western European poets. Modern Greek poets are liable to be anxious about their position in regard to Homer in a way which is uncharacteristic of Western poets. Knowing Homer in the rest of Europe is perceived rather as an accomplishment than as a patriotic duty; and major European languages have, unlike Greek, long had Moderns to pit against the Ancients. It is undeniable that Greece was fortunate enough to possess a 'national epic' from the distant past – unlike, say, the Czechs, who had to invent one – but the distance of that past must be conceded: to speak of 'the burden of the past' with respect to modern Greek poetry can be misleading if it prevents us from seeing that the modern Greek poet is in fact likely to want to burden himself with such a past for the advantages it may bring.[33] And because Homer's language does survive to some, however debatable, degree, the figure of Homer can only with great difficulty be seen as completely prediluvian, or allusion to Homer be as agreeably supererogatory for the modern Greek as it is for the foreign poet. The Greek educational system has until recent times imposed the teaching of the ancient language to the

[33] On the issue see briefly G. P. Savidis, 'The Burden of the Past and the Modern Greek Poet', *Grand Street* 4.2 (Winter 1985), 164–90.

exclusion of the modern in such a way as to leave those who have been part of it with strong feelings, one way or the other, about the ancient inheritance. Allusion to Homer can be non-committal, but it normally tends to indicate a degree of poetic ambition, even if this is reluctant to speak its name.

It would be wrong, however, to leave the reader with the impression from the start that Homer presents only anxieties and difficulties for his modern successor: great opportunities are presented too. In particular, the modern Greek poet whose most pressing task is to go beyond the achievements of his immediate precursors can often find in Homer the means to develop new or revive old resources of expression. We shall observe this self-renewing feature of modern Greek poetry in the case of Sikelianos, who goes back to Homer in order to stake a claim against his voluminous senior Palamas; in the case of Cavafy in relation to earlier poetry in Greek and English; and in the case of the modern 'most Homeric' poet, Seferis, as he makes his way in the face of his precursors earlier in the twentieth century. For all these poets, as Bate remarks with respect to the general problem of influence, Homer is 'ancestral rather than parental... remote enough to be more manageable in the quest for your own identity – more open to what the heart wants to select or the imagination to remould'.[34]

[34] Bate, *Burden*, p. 22.

PART ONE

HOMER IN THE NEW GREECE: THE SPIRIT AND THE LETTER

*

Chapter One
Kalvos and Solomos

I

> La nation contemple pour la première fois le spectacle hideux de son ignorance, et frémit en portant ses regards sur l'espace immense qui la sépare de la gloire de ses ancêtres.[1]

If modern Greece has an intellectual Founding Father it is without doubt Adamándios Koraïs (Coray) (1748–1833), a textual scholar of international renown and a liberal ideologue with a deep influence on the attitudes of independent Greece. The statement above, then, made at the time when the movement for Greek independence was taking root among the Greeks of the Diaspora, deserves serious attention. This book as a whole constitutes an effort to understand how modern Greek poetry has attempted to bridge the gap between itself and its ultimate poetic ancestor and model, Homer. It is far from surprising that Koraïs' nationalist pamphlet, *Martial Trumpet-Blast* (1803), has for its frontispiece a picture of Hellas as a woman in torn clothes – a Turk standing by with drawn sword – with a rag of parchment beneath her feet labelled 'HOMER'. Indeed, the picture bears the caption Ὤμοι ἐγὼ πανάποτμος, ἐπεὶ μ' ἕλε δούλιον ἦμαρ, a cento of two Iliadic lines: 'Alas for me most wretched, for the day of slavery is upon me.'[2]

The first poetic programme to bridge the gap between the moderns and the ancients that Koraïs felt so acutely was in fact inspired by his political and linguistic example. It was that of Andreas Kalvos, who published a collection of ten patriotic odes in Geneva in 1824

[1] A. Coray, *Mémoire sur l'état actuel de la civilisation dans la Grèce* (Paris 1803), p. 60 (repr. in Πολιτικὰ φυλλάδια τοῦ 'Αδαμαντίου Κοραῆ (Athens 1983)).

[2] Koraïs, Σάλπισμα πολεμιστήριον (Paris 1801), in Πολιτικὰ φυλλάδια.

and a further ten in Paris two years later. The occasion of these poems is the War of Independence, their idiom clearly influenced by Koraïs' efforts as a philologist to furnish the Greek people with a language fit for an enlightened Western nation.[3] But there is a further point, the significance of which is not always stressed with the force it deserves: Kalvos made a conscious decision to write his odes in Greek, which he knew, as a written language, imperfectly, rather than in the Italian in which his earliest poems are composed. In order to understand the importance of this decision we should turn our attention briefly to the most famous Greek poet of the early nineteenth century – Ugo Foscolo (1778–1827).

Foscolo, of course, wrote in Italian, not Greek, and it was at the age of only ten that he left his native island of Zante behind for ever. But it is Foscolo, in the absence of any other evidence for a connection between them, who forms an important link between those very different poets, Solomos and Kalvos. Kalvos, as Calbo, is familiar to Foscolians as the poet's amanuensis who moved to London with him in 1816; Solomos delivered an Italian funeral oration for Foscolo in Zante's Roman Catholic cathedral. The gentlemen of the Ionian Islands, which had for centuries been under Venetian rule but were now slipping from its grasp, were bilingual in Italian and Greek, but their intellectual world was definitely that of Italy. A Western education, often at Padua; a knowledge of the recent flowering of Italian poetry, which was far superior to anything written in Greek between the 1640s and the 1820s; a familiarity with at least the Latin classics: these were the foundations of the 'Ionian School'. Its very existence should make us the more careful in the discussion of the poetry of modern Greece; for it is, on the face of things, a paradox that the foundations of that poetry were laid outside the boundaries of the newly proclaimed state. Neither Solomos nor Kalvos ever lived in the Greek state – and Solomos never even visited it – but their decision to write in Greek, whatever the effort involved, had immediate patriotic motivation. It is possible that, had Foscolo been born a few years later than he was, he too would have made the attempt to write in Greek.

[3] K. Th. Dimarás, Ἑλληνικὸς ρωμαντισμός (Athens 1982), pp. 162–9.

As things are, we can see in the case of Foscolo that for him Hellas, in the particular form of Zante, was 'both a never-never dreamland *and* a concrete personal experience, the unrenounceable bond of birth'.[4] Take the sonnet that he wrote to his native island (1803):

> Nor shall I ever touch again the sacred shores
> where my body lay in childhood,
> my Zacynthus, who look into the waves
> of the Greek sea from which Venus was born,
>   virgin, and made these islands fecund
>   with her first smile, so that
>   your limpid clouds and your leaves
>   will not be passed over by the famous verse of him who sang
> the fatal waters and the diverse exile
> that was the lot of him who, fine in fame and sorrow,
> kissed his own rocky Ithaca – Ulysses.
>   You of your son shall have nothing but the song,
>   my motherland; to us fate has decreed
>   an unwept burial.[5]

Note, first of all, that the island is called here not Zante but the classicizing 'Zacinto'. Again, in this address to the island described by Homer as ὑλήεσσα ('woody') we find reference to its leaves, with an unnamed Homer assuming a place at the heart of the poem. The final words in particular (*illacrimata sepoltura*) are an echo, obvious to the educated reader, of the Odyssean phrase describing a dead man as ἄκλαυτος καὶ ἄθαπτος ('unwept and unburied'). Homer, in fact, was central to the mind of Foscolo: he exclaims in a letter of 1814, 'I am reading nothing but Homer, Homer, Homer.'[6] In 1807 he published an 'Experiment in the translation of the *Iliad* of Homer', and this project of translation continued through many vicissitudes to his death, leaving material that has now been edited into three substantial volumes.[7] Homer, for Foscolo, was both the celebrator of his native land (Ithaca is not far away) and the primal

[4] Glauco Cambon, *Ugo Foscolo. Poet of Exile* (Princeton 1980), p. 145.

[5] Text conveniently in Cambon, *Foscolo*, p. 42.

[6] Cambon, *Foscolo*, pp. 188–9.

[7] Ugo Foscolo, *Esperimenti di traduzione dell' Iliade* (3 vols., ed. G. Barbarisi, Florence 1961–7).

voice of poetry which provided a successor with a sense of vocation. One of the most memorable articulations of this sense is the final passage of 'Dei Sepolcri' (1807):

> Protect my fathers. One day you shall see
> a blind beggar wander among your
> most ancient shadows, and groping his way
> penetrate the burial chambers, and embrace the urns,
> and make question of them. The secret caves
> will groan, and the whole tomb will tell
> of Ilion twice razed and twice restored
> in splendour on the silent streets
> to make more fine the last trophy
> of Peleus' fated seed. The sacred bard,
> soothing those afflicted souls with song,
> will make eternal the Argive princes in as many
> lands as are embraced by great father Ocean.
> And you, Hector, will have the honour of tears
> wherever blood shed for country
> is sacred and bewailed, and as long as the Sun
> shines brightly on human sorrows.[8]

In this final peroration, which has come a long way from the poem's starting-point (a protest against the Napoleonic policy over the Paris cemeteries), Homer, on whom the poem has drawn in depth throughout, is not a disabling, but an enabling, presence for his successor. By so closely linking the figure of Homer himself to the *Iliad*, and in particular to its last line: 'So did they arrange the funeral of Hector, tamer of horses', Foscolo is faithful to Homeric poetry's view of its own purpose.[9] In attempting to establish Homer not only as their ancestor but as the ultimate source of their vocation, Foscolo's Greek juniors had a great deal to live up to.

II

Let us now return to Kalvos. His decision to write in Greek is an avowedly revivalist move: the poet's more conscious part, at least,

[8] Text in Tom O'Neill, *Of Virgin Muses and of Love. A Study of Foscolo's Dei Sepolcri* (Dublin 1981); with useful comments on the significance of Homer.

[9] Colin Macleod, 'Homer on Poetry and the Poetry of Homer', *Collected Essays* (Oxford 1983), pp. 1–15.

appears to believe that the Homeric letter *is* the spirit, that the modern Greek poet derives inspiration from the very words of Homer, much as Longinus judges in the case of the ancient authors. But the explicit references to Homer himself in Kalvos' odes are, perhaps unsurprisingly, among the more superficial elements in his poetry. Homer appears without great originality of character or expression among the Muses:

> Holy head
> of the divinely-inspired old man;
> happy voice which made famous
> the finest children
> of glorious Achaia,
>
> you, wonderful Homer,
> made the Muses welcome;
> and Zeus' daughters
> set on your lips
> the first honey.
>
> In honour of the gods
> you planted the laurel;
> many centuries saw
> the plant healthy,
> flourishing.

or in the company of other ancient worthies:

> There, you remember, you [Samos] filled
> the joyous bowl
> of Teian Anacreon,
> and strewed for the old man
> cool roses.
>
> There you taught Homer's
> fingers to run
> in harmony with the ode,
> as he told of deeds
> of gods and men.

There you inspired
the golden sayings of him [Pythagoras]
through whom the clouds were rent
and the stars' harmony
appeared to view.

Much closer to Kalvos' primary subject, the War of Independence, is this passage from the ode to Glory:

With his immortal measure
divine Homer cheered
the Achaean widows,
and your spirit was kindled
by the same melody.

You envied the fame
of the mighty Aeacides
(an ever-to-be-remembered, wonderful
envy) and spilt your blood
for Greece.[10]

Homer's presence here is not trivial or pointless: the revival of the memory of ancient Greece and the will to fight for a new Greece went hand in hand; the claim to an ancient inheritance that has long since passed to Europe does indeed require of the modern Greeks a response in action:

If we have the pride
to acquire it once again
with sweat and blood,
then well shall be the boast
of ancient glory.[11]

But the achievement of this revival in poetry will require comparable feats of endurance on the part of the poet: he will have to go beyond the customary references to the person of Homer. As proof of the presence of Homer as a shaping force – something which we can fairly claim to have found in the case of Foscolo – we shall demand

[10] Andréas Kálvos, Ὠδαί (ed. F. M. Pontani, Athens 1970), nos. V.91–105, XIV.31–45, II.61–70.

[11] Kalvos, Ὠδαί XIV.116–20.

more than just 'continuous reference to ancient names, places and pictures'.[12]

It is in his experimental translation of the beginning of Book 3 of the *Iliad*, an idea evidently inspired by Foscolo, that Kalvos comes closest to reviving the very words of Homer, as we can see by comparing the original and the translation: quoting the two together is an important exercise because it gives us an idea of the realism or otherwise of modern Greek revivalist ambitions in poetry.

Αὐτὰρ ἐπεὶ κόσμηθεν ἅμ' ἡγεμόνεσσιν ἕκαστοι,
Τρῶες μὲν κλαγγῇ τ' ἐνοπῇ τ' ἴσαν, ὄρνιθες ὥς,
ἠύτε περ κλαγγὴ γεράνων πέλει οὐρανόθι πρό,
αἵ τ' ἐπεὶ οὖν χειμῶνα φύγον καὶ ἀθέσφατον ὄμβρον,
κλαγγῇ ταί γε πέτονται ἐπ' Ὠκεανοῖο ῥοάων,
ἀνδράσι Πυγμαίοισι φόνον καὶ κῆρα φέρουσαι·
ἠέριαι δ' ἄρα ταί γε κακὴν ἔριδα προφέρονται·
οἱ δ' ἄρ' ἴσαν σιγῇ μένεα πνείοντες Ἀχαιοί,
ἐν θυμῷ μεμαῶτες ἀλεξέμεν ἀλλήλοισι.

Ἔπειτ' ἀφ' οὗ διετάχθησαν | ὑπὸ τοὺς ἡγεμόνας
ἅπαντες, με' φωνὰς | καὶ με' κτύπον ὡς ὄρνεα
κινοῦνται οἱ Τρῶες· ὡσαύτως | ὁ οὐρανὸς ἀκούει
ἐναερίους κλαγγὰς | ὅτε τὴν πολλὴν φεύγοντες
βροχὴν καὶ τὸν χειμῶνα | οἱ γερανοὶ διαβαίνουσι
τῆς θαλάσσης τὰ κύματα | μακρά, καὶ εἰς τὰ πυγμαῖα
ἔθνη, με' τῆς αὐγῆς | τὸ φῶς, φέρνουσι φόνον,
φέρνουν πικρὴν διχόνοιαν | καὶ πολύστονον μοῖραν.
Οἱ δ' Ἀχαιοὶ με' σιγὴν | πολλὴν πνέοντες δύναμιν,
καὶ εἰς ἀμοιβαῖαν βοήθειαν | δεινοί, πρόθυμοι ἐχώρουν.

(*But when each group had been put in order with its commanders, the Trojans went forth with calls and shouts, like birds, just like the calling of cranes before the heavens, who, on fleeing winter storms and abundant rain, fly with calls over the stream of Ocean, bringing killing and death to the Pygmies; and air-borne they bring on evil strife – but the Achaeans went forth in silence, breathing might, determined in heart to defend one another.*)[13]

[12] Yeóryios Zóras, Ὁ Κάλβος καὶ τὸ ὁμηρικὸν χειρόγραφον τῆς Γενεύης (Athens 1969), pp. 5–6.

[13] Kalvos, Ὠδαί, p. 173.

It is no coincidence, I think, that Kalvos has chosen to translate that passage of Homer which gives most support to the claim of Greek superiority over Oriental indiscipline (I wonder if we may also detect here an implicit, and timely, warning against the dangers of divisions among the Greek forces of the '21); and it is easy to see that many of his renderings are taken *verbatim* from Homer. But the passage is only a short sample which gives us little idea what a complete modern Greek *Iliad* would be like, and its language is sufficiently close to Homer's that it leaves unresolved the question whether a modern Greek audience really needed Homer to be translated in the first place. It did, in fact, but the poetry of the new state was not yet ready for the task.[14]

And yet it is undoubtedly the case that in Kalvos' ode 'The Ocean', with which his 1824 collection concludes, and which is at once the most compendious and the most commanding thing he ever wrote, the poet enriched his verse with (often unobtrusive) allusions to Homer.[15] The very title Ὁ Ὠκεανός revives ancient, and most famously Homeric, mythology in which Ocean is the father of all the gods and a 'great strength' in his own right (*Iliad* 21.195). But the very beginning of the ode makes it clear that here Ocean is being associated with the cause of the Greeks in particular:

> Land, care of the gods,
> Greece, mother of heroes,
> my dear, sweet fatherland,
> a night of slavery has covered you,
> a night of centuries.

This notion of a night of slavery sets off the first third of the poem (stanzas 2–12) with its most distinctive feature: a long, complex and virtually self-sufficient simile which it would have been hard to conceive without the example of Homer. This simile is not a short one extended by a tail, but a quite different thing; and far from distracting from the poetic (and at the same time the patriotic) purpose, the device builds up an expectation, in this case of a Greek

[14] On this question, with reference to the translation of the *Iliad* by Alexander Pallis, see Ricks, 'Homer and Greek Poetry', pp. 41–53.

[15] Kalvos, «Ὁ Ὠκεανός», Ὠδαί x.

revival. Like Homer's similes, moreover, Kalvos' simile here opens a window on a wider world of peace: and it does so in phrases which echo Homer. At dawn, for example,

φαίνονται
τώρα τῶν φιλοπόνων
ἀνδρῶν τὰ ἔργα

('*there now appear to view the works of industrious men*')

echoing *Iliad* 12.283, ἀνδρῶν πίονα ἔργα ('the rich estates of men'), itself in a simile.

Later in the ode, moreover, the goddess Liberty appears on the scene like the Homeric gods at Troy:

Ἦλθ' ἡ θεά· κατέβη
εἰς τὰ παραθαλάσσια
κλειτὰ τῆς Χίου

('*The goddess came; she descended to the glorious shores of Chios*')

With the Homeric epithet κλειτά we have a hint, perhaps, that Chios is being mentioned not just for its sufferings in 1822 (ode 6) and their avenging by Kanáris (ode 13) but for its being a proverbial home of Homer. And when Ocean responds to Liberty's prayer for the Greeks in stanza 23 we have a palpable use of Homeric diction:

Εἶπε· κ' εὐθὺς ἀπάνω
εἰς τὰς ῥοὰς ἐχύθη
τοῦ 'Ωκεανοῦ, φωτίζουσα
τὰ νῶτα ὑγρὰ καὶ θεῖα
προφαντος λάμψις.

('*She spoke, and straightaway was poured on the floods of Ocean, illuminating the back* [*of the sea*] *liquid and divine, a light plain to see.*')

Here the phrases echo the Homeric παρ' 'Ωκεανοῖο ῥοάων ('by the floods of Ocean'), νῶτα θαλάσσης ('the sea's back'), ὑγρὰ κέλευθα ('the liquid ways'). And these Homeric words are very much to the poetic purpose: they bolster the final mention of Ocean (naval battle with the Turks is about to be joined in stanza 30), and the claim that he is the father of the Greeks. It is as if, by possessing the ancient language, and Homer's in particular, the modern Greeks will be able to reclaim all the ἀρετή (approximately, *virtù*) of the ancients – a claim which has often been made in earnest since 1821.

Kalvos' achievement in this Horatian ode is a considerable one: among other things, he suggests a role for Homer's words in the poetry of the new Greece. But his poetry – and here I adopt a phrase which Palamas used of Solomos – is an example of ancient-seeming propriety rather than the product of a deep acquaintance with the ancients, and it does not suggest an obvious way forward for his successors.[16] Above all, no way was found by Kalvos himself; he lived till 1869 without ever publishing another poem.

III

Let us now turn to the contrasting, and perhaps rival, poetic programme of Count Dionisios Solomos, who first came to the attention of the Greek reading public with his 'Hymn to Liberty' (Paris 1825), part of which is now the National Anthem of Greece. Once again the influence of Foscolo is clear. Solomos' funeral oration for the older poet appropriately shows its esteem for Foscolo and the Homeric translator Vincenzo Monti (1754–1828) in the following terms:

> And we, taking the image from Homer, excellently translated by the living poet [Monti], shall present the difference that exists between these two [Foscolo and Monti] and those others who, without wishing to imitate them, write well:
>
> Athena and Ares their leaders,
> both golden with golden garments, great,
> beautiful, as immortals, armed, even from afar
> could be distinguished; and you could see tiny the throng below.[17]

[16] Kostís Palamás, Ἅπαντα (Athens n.d.), vol. 2, pp. 26–7.

[17] Dionísios Solomós, Ἅπαντα (ed. Línos Polítis), vol. 2 (Athens 1968), p. 197.

Solomos was in fact an acquaintance of Monti, and references to Homer come naturally to him; but the nature of his relation to Homer can be misunderstood. Take the most famous relevant poem, which gives this book its title:

THE SHADE OF HOMER

(Fragment)

The moon shone dimly – peace
made all, all of nature still.
And from its deserted bed
the nightingale began its plaint;
all around, the night calm
echoed the sweet weeping;
suddenly a deep sleep seized me,
and before my eyes an old man appeared.

The old man was resting on the shore;
over his old, torn clothes
sweetly the breath of wind
scattered his few white hairs,
and towards the many stars of the aether
he rolled his extinguished eyes;
slowly he arose,
and as if still sighted drew near me.[18]

This piece in *ottava rima* is one of the earlier things that the poet wrote in Greek (1818–24); it was, significantly, its first editor, Iákovos Polilás (1826–98), who, as well as correcting the scansion and spelling of this abandoned effort, gave it the title it now possesses.[19] Not surprisingly, Greek critics from Polilas on have tried to play up the importance of Homer for Solomos; at the same time, however, it is noticeable that the above poem is a development of a certain Romantic image of Homer (perhaps, in this case, also from the early Latin poet Ennius) rather than in any sense a drawing on the Homeric poems themselves. Indeed, reference to Homeric, as to

[18] Solomos, «Ἡ σκιὰ τοῦ Ὁμήρου», Ἅπαντα vol. 1 (Athens 1979), p. 58.

[19] For the MS version see Solomos, Αὐτόγραφα ἔργα (ed. Linos Politis, Thessaloniki 1964), vol. 1, pp. 62–3.

other ancient, myth is conspicuous by its absence from the poetry of Solomos. What then is Homer's place there?

Here too we need to come to terms with the fact that writing in Greek was a matter of conscious decision. It is true that, in one way, this may have had a liberating effect on the Greek poet, since it removed him from direct competition with the illustrious Italians; but it also posed considerable technical challenges for one who wrote in Italian throughout his life and who, as his manuscripts show, often composed his ideas in Italian and then attempted – often without success – to transfer them into Greek. It appears that Solomos' poetic naturalization, like that of Kalvos, was a direct response to the revolution, the '21. One of the fragmentary poems of the poet's early years is illuminating in this respect, not least because it reminds us of the fate of national poets: to adapt what Randall Jarrell once wrote of Robert Frost, people seem to like Solomos' best poems almost as much as they like his worst ones. The poem's first editor introduces it with the following note: 'He imagines that in the wilderness he will hear the voice of Homer, who with his presence at once animates insensate nature':

> Every stream in love,
> every breeze pure,
> every tree inspired
> speaks with its rustling.
>
> And where the rocks
> are most alone and silent,
> you shall hear Μῆνιν ἄειδε ['Sing the wrath...']
> being sung to you by a voice.
>
> And for your part follow the verse
> ...in order to see
> if the blind poet
> knows your voice.[20]

As clearly as in 'The Shade of Homer' we see here an aspiration to the Homeric succession; but although the picture of inspiration here was to impress a later national poet, Palamas, the spirit of

[20] Solomos, Ἅπαντα vol. 1, p. 16.

Ossian (mentioned by name in an 'Ode to the Moon' of about the same date) and the letter of the *Iliad*'s first words – words hardly at home in this peaceful setting – make strange bedfellows, especially given the language and metre of the quoted words of Homer.[21] Not long before Solomos is to write his 'Dialogue', a plea, with Dante as model, for the Greek vernacular, he here admits in poetry the intrusion of a dead language: the words in question would be incomprehensible to the average Greek. The resulting mixture of idioms in fact reinforces the barrier between the modern poet and his ancestor; and the sense of this is the more vivid because Solomos has, by giving them their modern quantity (–⏑–⏑), forced the words out of their original dactylic mould (–⏑⏑) and into his trochees. Somehow the effect that this produces is far from serious; and it is diverting to see Tennyson doing the same thing a few years later, quite consciously, in a poem called 'An Idle Rhyme':

> But if you prate of 'In' and 'Out'
>   And Dan and Joe, whoe'er they be,
> Then οἱη φυλλων will I spout,
>   οἱη περ φυλλων γενεη.

The poet's editor comments: '"It is interesting to see how, in the few words of Greek, the poet follows English accent and not Greek quantity." Possibly T. intended, by misscanning, to give the effect of a threadbare tag.'[22] Certainly a threadbare tag is what Homer so often ends up as in modern Greek poetry, not least because it is customarily felt important to quote him in an original that not even the educated can quote correctly.

It is not hard to see that the myth of a Shade or persisting spirit of Homer which Solomos and Kalvos inaugurate for modern Greece is precisely that which a poetic tradition will require if it is not in any poetic sense under the shadow of Homer. If Homer's words no longer overshadow our own, that is, we shall have to summon up the blind bard himself, as a kind of stage property, to breathe those words again. Once again, recalling Foscolo's 'Tombs', we reflect

[21] For Ossian see Solomos' poem, « Ὠδὴ εἰς τὴ σελήνη», Ἅπαντα vol. 1, p. 57; for Palamas see his Ἅπαντα vol. 2, p. 394.

[22] *The Poems of Tennyson* (ed. Christopher Ricks, 2nd edition, London 1986), vol. 2, p. 92.

that the power of its final passage derives not from the mere presence of Homer himself but from the reader's memories of the *Iliad*. That Homer's *ipsissima verba* are not, on the whole, part of Solomos' poetic diction can be illustrated by the sole specimen of Homeric translation that survives in his manuscripts, the beginning of *Iliad* 18:

Ὣς οἱ μὲν μάρναντο δέμας πυρὸς αἰθομένοιο,
Ἀντίλοχος δ᾽ Ἀχιλῆι πόδας ταχὺς ἄγγελος ἦλθε.
τὸν δ᾽ εὗρε προπάροιθε νεῶν ὀρθοκραιράων
τὰ φρονέοντ᾽ ἀνὰ θυμὸν ἃ δὴ τετελεσμένα ἦεν·
ὀχθήσας δ᾽ ἄρα εἶπε πρὸς ὃν μεγαλήτορα θυμόν·
"ὤ μοι ἐγώ, τί τ᾽ ἄρ᾽ αὖτε κάρη κομόωντες Ἀχαιοὶ
νηυσὶν ἔπι κλονέονται ἀτυζόμενοι πεδίοιο;

Ἐπολεμοῦσαν ἔτσι ὡσὰν τὴ φλόγα·
Μηνυτὴς ἦλθε ὁ Ἀντίλοχος ὡστόσο
Γλήγορα ἐκεῖ στὸν Ἀχιλλέα· τὸν ηὗρε
Ὁπου ὀμπρὸς εἰς τὰ ὀρθόπρυμνα καράβια
Μὲ τὸ νοῦ του ὅ, τι ἐστάθη ἐμελετοῦσε·
Κ᾽ ἔλεε πικρῶς ἡ μεγάλη ψυχή του:
Συφορά! γιατί τάχα ὅλοι σκορπιοῦνται
Μὲ ἀντάρα εἰς τὸ πεδίον, καὶ φεύγουν ὅλοι
Τρομασμένοι οἱ Ἀχαιοὶ κατὰ τὰ πλοῖα;

(*So then they fought like blazing fire, but Antilochus swift of foot came as a messenger to Achilles. And he found him in front of the tall-prowed ships thinking in his heart of what had come to pass; and grieving he addressed his brave heart: 'Alas, why are the long-haired Achaeans beaten in retreat from the plain back against the ships?'*)[23]

Apart from the proper names, linguistic continuity here is attenuated: a glance at the page is sufficient to show this. Solomos has evidently recast Homer in a form of Italian derivation which owes much to the example of Monti. At this point we must set a preconception aside: that the fifteen-syllable 'political verse' is the metre in which any modern Greek Homer properly belongs. Although Solomos' editor and disciple, Polilas, used the metre in his

[23] Solomos, Ἅπαντα vol. 1, p. 316.

own Homeric translations, we need not infer that Solomos would have done the same; and again a parallel with Tennyson may be drawn. In the famous debate on Homeric translation between Matthew Arnold and F. W. Newman in the 1860s it was common ground that the length of blank verse disabled it from translating the much longer lines of Homer; but Tennyson perceived that it was only in a verse form fully cultivated by poetry at large, and not in a form devised especially for the purpose, that Homer could acquire the necessary dignity in the modern language; and so he experimented with translating Homer into blank verse, with impressive results (this passage is from *Iliad* 18.219–27):

> For like the clear voice when a trumpet shrills,
> Blown by the fierce beleaguerers of a town,
> So rang the clear voice of Æakides;
> And when the brazen cry of Æakides
> Was heard among the Trojans, all their hearts
> Were troubled, and the full-maned horses whirled
> The chariots backwards, knowing griefs at hand;
> And sheer-astounded were the charioteers
> To see the dread, unweariable fire
> That always o'er the great Peleion's head
> Burned, for the bright-eyed goddess made it burn.[24]

Of course, it takes more to recast Homer into blank verse than to trot along with him in the English hexameter or the Greek 'political verse'. But Solomos gives us a sign that he might have been able to surmount the challenge in the single memorable line (noted by Seferis),

Καὶ γυμνὸ στὴ σφαγὴ τὸν ποδοσέρνει

('*and he drags him naked by the foot into the slaughter*')

Here we have encapsulated the *Iliad* as 'le poème de la force', in Simone Weil's phrase.[25]

Solomos' involvement with Homer did in fact go much further than this solitary specimen of translation: his acquaintance with the

[24] Tennyson, *Poems* vol. 2, p. 656.

[25] The line in Solomos, Ἅπαντα vol. 1, p. 317; quoted in George Seferis, Μέρες vol. 5 (repr. Athens 1977), p. 64.

Iliad and the *Odyssey* in Italian translation was profound; and the fact that he was largely unacquainted with Homeric Greek evidently helped him to concentrate on the meaning of the poems instead of being overcome with *frissons* over the linguistic surface, something to which Greeks can be prone. We can see from Polilas' 'Prolegomena' to the poems and from elsewhere that Solomos had an eye for the strengths of Homer; but our concern here is whether these concerns find expression, however fragmentarily, in poetic practice.[26] Let us note briefly two contrasting examples.

The poem 'On Márkos Bótsaris' was written, it appears, immediately after the death of the hero outside the besieged Missolonghi in August 1823. Solomos, in Zante to the south west, could hear the cannons: events had put a second Troy in his mind. Hence the following stanzas:

> The remains that Priam
> had secured through laments, through gifts,
> were returning at the hour
> when the sweet light of dawn
> falls to the face of earth.
>
> There came out together from all parts
> of grieving Troy
> women, children and old men,
> lamenting the sight of the corpse
> that lays down its life for them.
>
> No mouth remained closed
> over the body of Markos;
> dead, dead is Markos;
> an affliction, a shout of extremity,
> a lament and much weeping.[27]

Here Homer's world and the contemporary world are made one through the easy paratactic transition between the second and third stanzas; the word for lament (θρῆνος) as well as the thing can be

[26] For Solomos' Homeric interests see the 'Prolegomena' by Iakovos Polilas (Solomos, Ἅπαντα vol. 1, p. 31) and N. B. Tomadákis, «Ὁ Σολωμὸς καὶ οἱ ἀρχαῖοι», Νεοελληνικά. Δοκίμια καὶ μελέται Β′ (Athens 1983), pp. 7–32.

[27] Solomos, «Εἰς Μάρκο Μπότσαρη», Ἅπαντα vol. 1, pp. 137–8 (date on p. 347).

traced right back to the relevant passage of the *Iliad* (24.721); and the poet's belief is confirmed that

> the foreigner comes and finds still living many customs of the *Iliad*: women still say dirges over the dead and kiss them. The old man in his grief still strikes his forehead with his two hands, and raises them to the skies, as if wishing to ask them why so great a misfortune has befallen him... The mother still bares her breast to remind her child of the milk she gave it.[28]

This way of thinking, by which contemporary events are seen as repeating the events of the *Iliad*, and are thereby lent a further dignity, is taken a stage further in Solomos' ambitious and unfinished composition, 'The Free Besieged'. A passage from the poet's working notes that has been cited by Kakridis in order to shed light on the development of the plot of the *Iliad* can speculatively be reversed so as to illustrate Solomos' relation to Homer:

> The women, who up to that point have shown greatness of heart comparable to that of the men, are, when it is their turn to pray, somewhat afraid and weep, by which the Action is advanced; because all the behaviour of the women has its effect on the hearts of the warriors, and that is the last external force that militates against them, from which, as from all the others, they emerge free.[29]

The emphasis here on women and their role sets Solomos' use of the *Iliad* apart from contemporary attempts (discussed below) to read Homer in the light of the klefts, the modern bandits-turned-freedom-fighters. But the Homeric poems themselves go unmentioned. In utter contrast to Kalvos, Solomos has learned from Homer – and especially about the *vivida vis* of great poetry – but takes to be part of this lesson the exclusion of overt references to Homer or the Homeric poems. Homer is perhaps the most important part of a valued, but unrevivable, ancient past.

[28] Solomos, Ἅπαντα vol. 2, p. 23.

[29] Solomos, Ἅπαντα vol. 1, p. 229; comments in J. Th. Kakridis, *Homer Revisited* (Lund 1971), p. 114.

Chapter Two
Archaism and kleftism

I

Validating their claims as rightful heirs of Homer required more of the modern Greek poets than simply banishing the Turks and what Kalvos called their 'blasphemous measures'.[1] But the important examples of Kalvos and Solomos were largely ignored over the next half-century, in respect of Homeric allusion among other things. Kalvos had shown, intermittently, that drawing on Homeric language could have poetic as well as patriotic substance, provided that such borrowings were subordinated to a strong form; Solomos had reminded the reader, fragmentarily, that a mind familiar with the Homeric poems was a mind enriched. Kalvos, to put it epigrammatically, had shown the use of the Homeric letter, Solomos that of the Homeric spirit. Their Athenian contemporaries and juniors, however – at a time, admittedly, when the Greek state was subject to severe constitutional and cultural uncertainties – failed to incorporate Homer in their poetry except at the most superficial level. In any case, Solomos and, especially, Kalvos were not names to conjure with in Athens. Although they are now seen as the founders of modern Greek poetry, we can see from a well-known anthology of 1841, for example, that they were not only less prolific but also less esteemed than the poets of the Athenian School.[2]

Now the Athenian School is best known (and least read) today for its characteristic archaizing idiom – an attempt, in some cases, virtually to recreate ancient Greek – and one might expect that a more thorough-going version of Kalvos' revivalism might have been set in motion, whereby Homeric diction would be the foundation of a new poetry. But this was in fact recognized as a non-starter even by the archaizing judges of the prestigious Rállis Poetry Competition of 1857, who protested that 'The extensive use of Homeric words in all three of these poems is utterly pointless, since

[1] Kalvos, Ὠδαί XIII.55.

[2] K. A. Hantserís, Ἑλληνικὸς Νέος Παρνασσός (Athens 1841).

it is obviously impossible to resurrect the old Achaeans of the Trojan age to read and enjoy them.'[3] A significant feature of the Athenian poetry of the mid-century is indeed its frank recognition that the letter of Homer had been passed on to the West, and that it was by Westward intellectual movement that Greece would recover its spiritual heritage: in a famous sonnet (1845) Stéfanos Kumanúdis (1818–99) reminded readers that it had been Venice (through its Greek presses) which had enlightened Greece during her dark age.[4] Other Athenian poets, however, perceived a still more imposing barrier between Homer and themselves. The realities of the new Greek state were not such as to permit complacency that Homer's world had been resurrected; hence these lines by Aléksandros Sútsos (1803–63) from a poem entitled 'The Ruins of Troy' (1836):

The memory of the great Hellenic past.
The comparison with our humble, wretched present.

A later Romantic poet, Spirídon Vasiliádis (1845–94), laments the absence of inspiration in these terms (1872):

Homer's word no longer pours forth,
but the string groans out of tune.

Finally, in a passage of greater complexity (1867), Dimítrios Paparrigópulos (1843–73) treats the pre-Christian age of Homer as a Golden Age of happiness; the lines are worth quoting because, like the rest of the poem in which they appear, they are preoccupied with the themes of ageing and mortality which we shall find to be so prominent in Cavafy's reading of Homer.

Homer, your merry, pious heart,
taking various fragments of traditions,
remoulded Olympus for society,
and the Muse creates the gods anew.

But you made them too, too lovely,
and Olympus was but joy's protector,
and you imagined mortals as blessed, in their prime;
to whom may grief tell its sadness?

[3] In Dimaras, Ἑλληνικὸς ρωμαντισμός, p. 203; see also p. 535.
[4] In G. P. Savidis, Πάνω νερά (Athens 1973), pp. 57–8.

Most striking is the cry, 'Homer, mankind is not rejoicing, not now.'[5]

Now this romantic outlook has, admittedly, little to do with the Homeric poems; but we can see from the above examples that this school of poetry, if it comes into contact with Homer at all, is inclined to bewail the absence of Homer rather than to celebrate his presence in the new Greece. The sense that there is something which for ever separates us moderns from Homer was expressed as late as 1904 by these poets' more famous successor, Kostis Palamas. In his poem 'Ascraeus' he adopts the *persona* of Hesiod and indeed explicitly distances himself from possible claims to being a Homer:

> The blind rhapsode of Olympus, divine Melesigenes,
> calmly hymns mortals, heroes, gods.
> You, my song, come out of an uneasy spring,
> and you are always lava and sea-swell.
> Listen, I am the Ascraean; I am not the craftsman
> of peaceful golden dreams, of glad tunes;
> the magnet of the black earth on which I tread draws me,
> my mind goes with the wings of sighs.[6]

It appears, then, that Homer is characteristically mentioned in order to express some sense of alienation; but there were prominent attempts to bring Homer into the poetry of the present. In this connection the verse prologue by A. R. Rangavís (Rangabé) (1809–92) to his translation of the first book of the *Odyssey* (1840) is revealing. The poet mournfully compares the state of Homeric learning in Greece and in the West in Homeric hexameters that deserve to be quoted for their dottiness:

> the oaks of Teutonia whisper his melodies now,
> and Albion understands the bard of soft Ionia,
> but in Hellas his voice is silent.

Rangavis goes on to clarify what he means: that whereas Homer has been understood by the Germans and the English (and become

[5] Quotations from Hantseris, Παρνασσός, p. 69 and Δ. Παπαρρηγόπουλος–Σ. Βασιλειάδης (Βασική Βιβλιοθήκη) (Athens 1954), pp. 225 and 52–3.

[6] Palamas, «Ἀσκραῖος», Ἅπαντα vol. 3, p. 203.

naturalized through Voss and Pope), he is in Greece just a text (κείμενον) which has not been brought back to life:

> The psalmist lies before us, but not like a bird of the Graces,
> warbling a sweet song, and setting alight and bewitching the mind,
> but like a gigantic corpse which a pedant anatomizes
> in cold blood, researching dialects and accidence and metres.[7]

It would be hard to dispute that it has been Homer's fate to be murdered at the hands of Greek schoolmasters: even the excellent translator of Homer, Alexander Pállis (1851–1935), recalled late in life how much he had hated doing Homer at school.[8] But the main means by which Rangavis seeks to resuscitate Homer for a modern Greek audience seems inadequate: it is his use of the Homeric hexameter. A younger poet, Theódoros Orfanídis (1817–1886), quotes with approval Rangavis' lines.

> When ancient Greece is resurrected, and with it the ancient
> sensibility, with it must be resurrected its ancient verse too.[9]

But it is an open secret that extreme archaism in poetry backfires if the aim is to produce poetry of classical decorum; and Rangavis' metre is to be seen rather as a substitute for the ancient hexameter's powers of expression, no more than a strange *simulacrum* of Homeric verse. In the same decade in England, Arthur Hugh Clough used the hexameter to colloquial and comic effect in 'The Bothie of Tober-na-Vuolich' (1848), but a tongue-in-cheek attitude to the form was perhaps too much to ask of the Greeks so soon after Independence, and the modern Greek hexameter continued to be in vogue: Orfanidis' poem in the metre, 'Chios Enslaved', won the Poetry Competition of 1858. Looking at its opening lines, it is easy to see that they have a vague archaic flavour without actually having roots in the Homeric poems themselves at all:

> When he is sailing towards the shores of Asia Minor, the sailor
> comes on a glad island not far from blessed Smyrna;
> though a fragrant atmosphere of lovely scents bathes it,

[7] A. R. Rangavís, Ἅπαντα τὰ φιλολογικά (Athens 1874), vol. 2, pp. 205–7.

[8] Aléksandros Pállis, Μπρουσός (ed. E. Moschonás, Athens 1975), p. 34n.

[9] Theódoros Orfanídis, Ἅπαντα (Athens 1915), p. 153.

> it is not the island of the Blest ... at the season of spring,
> when the deep seas and mountains are silent and nature slumbers;
> though mysterious sounds emanate from it,
> it is not the habitation of dangerous mythical Sirens.
>
> Hail Chios; if not the birthplace of great Homer,
> the land where he might have imagined Olympus and sung with enthusiasm!
> Beneath Mount Aipos I reverently grasped the rock by the sea
> where the fertile mind of ancient Greece used to sit,
> and in the silence of the night my alert ear heard
> with the most sacred harmony of the shining stars
> the quickening echo of the blind Muse-inspired poet's epics.[10]

This rooting of Homer to the famous *Daskalópetra* ('Rock of the Teacher') in Chios is very far from an indication that in this poem we have in any sense a continuation of the tradition of Homer. And the neglected archaizing poetry of this period, much of which is not without merit, is best regarded – like the use of classical metres in English poetry – as an experiment which is anything but conservative. Rangavis' 'The Voyage of Dionysus' (1864), for example, is a minor masterpiece, to which we may happily apply Eliot's remarks on Swinburne:

> the object has ceased to exist ... the meaning is merely the hallucination of meaning, because language, uprooted, has adapted itself to an independent life of atmospheric nourishment ... The bad poet dwells partly in a world of objects and partly in a world of words, and he can never get them to fit. Only a man of genius could dwell so exclusively and consistently among words as Swinburne.[11]

But 'The Voyage of Dionysus', significantly, is derived from a classical Athenian source, not from the Homeric poems, and this is a feature of the Athenian School in general: Homer is much less important for these poets than we might have suspected. Even English thought at this time is very much centred round fifth-

[10] In Linos Politis (ed.), Ποιητική ἀνθολογία (Athens 1975), vol. 4, pp. 126–7.
[11] Eliot, *Sacred Wood*, p. 149.

century Athens, and it is not surprising to find that this is still more true of the new Athens itself.[12] Above all, there is a general point about the literary culture which was made by Seferis:

> When, e.g., a 'great flatterer' – as Michael Psellus tells us – whispers to Augusta Sclyraena the start of the famous verse of the *Iliad* about Helen οὐ νέμεσις [3.156–7: 'it is no reproach for the Trojans and well-greaved Achaeans long to suffer ills over such a woman as this'], I feel the presence of Homer far more alive in those years of Christian Byzantium than in the antiquity-obsessed Athens of 1860, where, in spite of the endless racket about them, the ancients are nowhere to be found.[13]

Seferis' point can be glossed: it is not just that the Athenians of 1860 never even approached the spirit of Homer, it is that they were not even that familiar with the letter. The characteristic mode of allusion in this period of modern Greek poetry above all others is simply proverbial. It consists of mottoes – which require no knowledge of Homeric context or content – extraneous to the body of the new poem in which they appear; as we shall find when we come to look at the poetic background to Cavafy. Allusion of this kind can only be facile – it deals with absolutely unresisting material – and the poetic rewards are meagre.

II

There was, however, a completely different way of exploiting Homer which exerted no little influence on Greek poetry in the second half of the nineteenth century: this intuitively attractive but ultimately rather narrow interpretation of the Homeric spirit as being the national property of the modern Greeks may be termed 'kleftism'. I take the word from Michael Herzfeld, who has provided us with an iconoclastic account of how the klefts, the bandits who in earlier times harried their Ottoman masters, threw in their lot with the War of Independence ('the '21') and became an important part

[12] Dimaras, Ἑλληνικὸς ρωμαντισμός, pp. 204–5.
[13] Seferis, Δοκιμές (Athens 1974), vol. 2, p. 179.

of the ideology of the independent state.[14] It was tempting to take a step beyond this foundation-myth and to link the klefts with the Homeric heroes they in some ways resembled: this would at once make the modern heroes Homeric and the Homeric poems distinctively the voice of the Greek race. Even the extreme archaist scholar George Mistriótis (1840–1916) wrote in 1871, with a revealing sense of priorities, 'Each hero of the time of the Klefts and each commander of our great Revolution is the most comprehensive and most eloquent scholium on the Homeric epics.'[15] And another professor, Fílippos Ioánnu (1796–1880), produced one of the most bizarre cultural manifestations of modern Greece when he translated into pseudo-Homeric Greek a bogus folk song:

> μῆτερ' ἐμὴ τριφίλητ', ὠμόφροσιν οὐκέτι Τούρκοις
> δουλεύειν δύναμαι· τέτρυταί μοι κέαρ ἔνδον.
>
> ('*Dear mother, I can no longer be a slave to the cruel Turks; my heart is anguished within.*')[16]

The temptation to relate Homer and the world of the klefts as expressed in the folk songs known as 'kleftic songs' lay first and foremost in the continuing identity of the natural world of Greece and the sort of manners it nurtured. Palamas cited a passage of Goethe as a contrast to the Greek's experience of things:

> The rest of us, men of dry land and inhabitants of the interior, are indeed bewitched by the reading of the *Odyssey*; but what impresses us most fully and uniquely is the poem's ethical and psychological significance, whereas our imagination can only succeed imperfectly and with great effort in being held by its descriptive parts.[17]

The Greek could feel that he was familiar with the homes of the heroes: in particular, the original Thessalian Hellas of Achilles

[14] Michael Herzfeld, *Ours Once More: Folklore, Ideology and the Making of Modern Greece* (Austin 1982).

[15] G. Mistriótis, Κρίσις τοῦ Βουτσιναίου Ποιητικοῦ Ἀγῶνος τοῦ ἔτους 1871 (Athens 1871).

[16] In J. E. Sandys, *A History of Classical Scholarship* (London 1908), vol. 3, p. 374; the charge that the song was bogus anyway by N. G. Polítis, «Γνωστοὶ ποιηταὶ δημοτικῶν ᾀσμάτων», Λαογραφικὰ σύμμεικτα vol. 1 (Athens 1920), pp. 211–36.

[17] Palamas, Ἅπαντα vol. 12, p. 354.

himself was now part of the new Hellas, just. But identifying the two heroic worlds of ancient and modern folk song was a larger step and a questionable one.

Claude Fauriel mentioned Homer in the preface to his path-breaking collection of folk songs (vol. 1, Paris 1824), and folk song came to be talked of in the same breath as Homer; but not always in the most convincing terms.[18] In the German scholar Passow's treatise on the Homeric simile (1852), for example, we find the fairly gratuitous comment, evidently inspired by the klefts: 'the whole life of the *Iliad* and the *Odyssey* breathes freedom, and the δούλιον ἦμαρ ['day of slavery'] or the ἐλεύθερον ['day of freedom'] will not come without bloodshed'. In the preface to his large collection of folk songs a few years later (1860), the same scholar gave the point fuller expression:

> But moreover, antiquaries will find not a few things in these folk songs that are worthy of attention, such as that Charon, the deities of rivers and trees, and Fate are still customarily venerated by the Greeks as gods. But you shall wonder all the more at the fact that blind rhapsodes wandering round the villages, like those who some thirty centuries ago sung of the adventures of Odysseus and the battles of Achilles, to this very day customarily entertain the populace on feast days with epic songs. The deeds of the klefts, who resisted their Turkish rulers for many years with great fortitude, seem to these men no less worthy of being celebrated in song than the great exploits of the Achaeans did to those.[19]

The quaintness of these passages is greatly increased when we reflect that they appear here translated from the original Latin.

A later generation better informed about Greek popular life would see that these blind rhapsodes were a myth.[20] And this was not the only problem which the klefts presented for an ideology which was attempting to put them in a Homeric mould. In the first place, they were never a Panhellenic phenomenon, being restricted

[18] Claude Fauriel, *Chants populaires de la Grèce moderne* vol. 1 (Paris 1824), p. xxxix.

[19] A. Passow, *de comparationibus homericis* (Berlin 1852), p. 9; (ed.), Τραγούδια ρωμαίικα – *Carmina popularia Graeciae recentioris* (Leipzig 1860), pp. v–vi.

[20] N. G. Politis, «Γνωστοὶ ποιηταί».

to certain areas of central and northern Greece; more disturbingly, as banditry obstinately survived the establishment of the free state, doubts could be cast on the klefts' enlightened credentials. Even so, the kinship of the klefts and Homeric heroes lived on as a critical commonplace. The iconoclastic author of *Pope Joan*, Emmanuíl Roïdis (1836–1904), uses the cliché for characteristically ironical purposes in an essay of 1877:

> If the opinion of a number of contemporary critics be supposed correct, that the armatoles of the period of Turkish rule are to be considered more similar to the ancient heroes than are the [medieval] knights, and the anonymous singers of the Pindus and Mount Olympus more Homeric than the troubadours, then in that case our country is left with the fame that it was not only the cradle but the grave of the heroic life, from Odysseus Laertou to Odysseus Androutsos.[21]

This latter was a happy coincidence of name between an ancient and a modern hero, but General Makriyánnis (1797–1864) had a plain man's scepticism about all these ancient names; he writes in his memoirs of the period,

> And you made a new commander in the garrison at Corinth, Achilles he was called, a man of learning; and on hearing the name Achilles you expected that it was the famous Achilles; and it was the name that was fighting the Turks.[22]

Rejection of the revival of ancient names could, however, be carried out in a spirit of positive pride and self-assertiveness; take this letter of 1878 by the influential poet and politician Aristotélis Valaorítis (1821–79):

> Homer sang the klefts of that time, who were superior to those of modern times only insofar as they were fortunate enough to have a divine bard. Therefore I worship him. In place of his heroes' names I substitute in my imagination the names of Kúmas, Pános Meidánis, Vlahangélis, Sumalás,

[21] E. D. Roïdis, Ἅπαντα (ed. A. Angélou, Athens 1978), vol. 2, p. 287.
[22] In Seferis, Δοκιμές vol. 1, pp. 235–6.

> Hrístos Valaóras, Astrapóyannos, Konstandáras, Díplas, Katsandónis, and I reach the point of believing that the race has remained unaltered, unadulterated, immortal.

In Valaoritis' view, this has implications for poetic practice:

> My prejudice has reached such a point that even those glorious Hellenic names I consider to be incompatible with the harmony of the verse, and in writing 'Athanásios Diákos' I found myself unable to introduce anywhere in the poem either Thermopylae or Leonidas.[23]

Here we undoubtedly have a sense of a modern Greek identity and poetic not beholden to Homer and the ancients.

But we have yet to consider the fundamental difficulty in relating the Homeric and the kleftic worlds: the generic difference between Homeric epic and folk songs. How can we regard as commensurate with the former a corpus of songs few in number, small in scale and in technique relatively primitive? We shall have to be talking about the 'Homeric spirit' in a very vague sense.[24] There are, indeed, illuminating affinities and points of comparison between the *Iliad* and the kleftic songs, as Kakridis has shown – but justice had to be done to the Homeric poems by the refusal to read them simply as folk songs writ large if the klefts' relation to Homer was to prove profitable to the modern Greek poets.[25] As early as 1833, before 'kleftism' had taken full hold of the Greek mind, Solomos had presciently warned that the poet could not settle for reproducing the kleftic poetry; and the point has particular application to those poets who would allude to a Homer now so commonly thought of in 'kleftic' terms:

> I am glad that they are taking folk songs as their starting point; but I should like whoever uses the kleftic language to do so in its essence, and not formally, do you understand me? And as for writing poetry, attend to this ... certainly it is well to put down one's roots upon these traces but not to stop

[23] Ἀριστοτέλης Βαλαωρίτης (ed. G. P. Savidis *et al.*, Athens 1980–1), vol. 1, pp. 322–3 and vol. 2, p. 329.

[24] See R. M. Dawkins in *Journal of Hellenic Studies* 54 (1934), 106–7.

[25] See e.g. Kakridis, *Homer Revisited*, pp. 143–6.

> there: one must rise perpendicularly. Kleftic poetry is fine and interesting as an ingenuous manifestation by the klefts of their lives and thoughts and feelings. It does not have the same interest on our lips; the nation requires from us the treasure of our individual intelligence, clothed in national forms.[26]

III

At the birth of the new Hellas, Solomos and Kalvos each suggested ways in which the poetry of the nation could make something of the Homeric inheritance – could make the case that it was an inheritance at all. But despite the lip-service paid to Homer, as to the ancients generally, Homer was of very limited importance for the poetry of the years that followed compared with various influences from Western Europe. In fact the sole memorable poem of this half-century or so that has anything much to do with Homer is, ironically, a parody: the 'Row between Agamemnon and Achilles' (1872) by the Cephalonian Andréas Laskarátos (1811–1901); here the incongruity of finding latter-day Greeklings in the great world of Homer is evident in the very title. The poem follows quite closely the episode in Book 1 of the *Iliad* – but with deviations from the tone that we should expect a translation to adopt: take these lines based on part of a speech of Achilles (*Iliad* 1.149–71):

> Did I come to Troy
> out of a grudge of my own against the Turks, eh?
> What have the Trojans done to me?
> Nothing, to be sure; no, I came for you,
> fatty, skinflint, excommunicant, Mason;
> and for your cuckold brother.[27]

Through the deliberate confusion of two worlds, reflected particularly in the contrast between the Homeric proper names and the Ionian Islands dialect and society of 1870, both the Homeric and the contemporary worlds are mocked; we are to deduce that Aga-

[26] A letter to Yeóryios Tertsétis, here quoted from Roderick Beaton, *Folk Poetry of Modern Greece* (Cambridge 1980), p. 8.

[27] Andréas Laskarátos, «Καβγᾶς μεταξὺ ᾿Αγαμέμνονος καὶ ᾿Αχιλέως [sic]», Ποιήματα (ed. E. Moschonás, Athens 1981), p. 125.

memnon and Achilles were no better than today's politicians. This *jeu d'esprit* is carried out neatly within a strong local tradition of verse satire and invective. Opposed to the irredentist Great Idea (for which Homer provided part of the inspiration), opposed to the Union of the Ionian Islands with Greece in 1864, Laskaratos still mentally inhabits a world in which it is possible to treat Homer as one wishes without thereby making any considered poetic statement.

Chapter Three
Palamas

Kostis Palamas is a various as well as a voluminous poet, and it would be surprising if his work was not replete with references to Homer and the Homeric poems. A look at the index to the collected works of Palamas, on the other hand, reveals that Byron takes up as much space as Homer, Goethe and Victor Hugo very much more; and it cannot be maintained that the presence of Homer is central to the poetry of Palamas as it is, say, to that of Seferis.[1] And yet, in order to understand Palamas' successors the better, we must look synoptically at the importance of Homer for his poetry.

Born in Patras and brought up in Missolonghi, Palamas was aware from an early date that his native locality, physically and culturally, looked rather towards the Ionian Islands than towards the capital, Athens. As a poet, he came to express a debt – at once envy and allegiance – to those islands that had in the mythical past produced Odysseus and had in the years shortly before Palamas' birth nurtured Solomos. The following passage which Palamas wrote about Corfu makes the feeling clear enough:

> the Homeric song holds there more firmly than elsewhere its distinctive characteristics ... the Homeric harmony is revealed in a more lively fashion in the light which animates and the peace that relaxes the physical beauties there ... does not the poetry of Homer spread out like an intellectual heaven over the air of the place in which Solomos chose to live? ... Superior are the poets of the Heptanese, heirs to the lyre of Demodocus, which gladdened the hearts of the Phaeacians and brought tears to the eyes of Odysseus.[2]

Palamas is of course making the familiar identification of the mythical island of Scheria with Corfu, to which Solomos moved in 1828 and where he wrote his best poetry; and he develops this sense of the

[1] The index is vol. 17 of the Ἅπαντα: Εὑρετήρια (ed. G. P. Savidis and G. Kehayóglu, Athens 1984).

[2] Palamas, Ἅπαντα vol. 2, pp. 26–33.

Ionian Islands' Homeric connections in a sonnet in the sequence 'Homelands' (1895):

> There where Homer's Phaeacians are still living,
> and East with a kiss mingles with West,
> and with the olive flowers everywhere the cypress,
> deep-coloured adornment of the azure of the Infinite,
>
> there my soul desired to live a sweet life
> with the great rocky view of the land of Pyrrhus,
> there where the manna of dawn, the spring of harmony,
> pour down like beauties in a dream.
>
> There with a new Greek voice the rhapsodies
> of the immortal Blind One wisely echo,
> there the scents of roses are breathed
>
> by the shade of Solomos in Elysium, and there
> the craftsman of the lyre lives again, and Demodocus
> hymns the land and glory of Crete.[3]

This is an allusive poem, and one or two points are worth glossing in order to indicate how Palamas understands his relation to Homer: here he is commending a tradition to which he does not himself really belong. Homer's rhapsodies echo in Corfu with 'a new Greek voice' because in 1881 Polilas has completed his translation of the *Odyssey* into the native idiom of his mentor Solomos. The celebrator of the Shade of Homer himself has been honoured by the depiction of his shade in Elysium; more unexpectedly, the last clause is a tribute to Cretan poetry. It was in the rhyming couplets perfected by the Cretan Renaissance poets that a successor of Solomos, Yerásimos Markorás (1826–1911), had written his poem Ὁ Ὅρκος ('The Oath') about the Cretan rising of 1866.[4] The ancestors of Solomos were themselves Cretans who had moved to Zante after the capture of Candia in 1669. It is evident that a good deal of literary history is packed into these lines.

This early poem appears to offer Palamas plenty of material that might later be developed in order to accord to Homer a central

[3] Palamas, Ἅπαντα vol. 3, p. 16.

[4] Yerásimos Markorás, Ἅπαντα (Athens n.d.), pp. 7–54.

place; and yet Homer never acquires this place. Nonetheless, two poems from Palamas' major lyric collection *The Unstirring Life* (1904), though they are far from being his best work, illuminate aspects of the problem of Homeric allusion which we shall find useful when we come to look at Sikelianos and Seferis. The first is a poem called Ραψωδία ('Rhapsody') (1897):

Divine Homer, joy and glory of the ages!
In the school's chill and on the bench's bareness,
when the teacher's graceless hands
placed you before me, o book of great joy,
I was expecting you as a lesson and you came as a miracle.
And within me opened up a broad, clear sky
and a deep sea's sapphire scattered with emeralds,
and it was as if the bench became a palace's throne
and the school a world and the teacher a prophet.
This was not reading, not understanding:
it was vision and hearing without peer.—
In the great cave surrounded by
a dense wood of poplars and cypresses,
in the great cave with its scent
and its warmth from the cedar fire,
bright-haired Calypso no longer weaves
with golden shuttle, no longer sings
with fine voice; raising her hands the nymph
scatters a curse from a flaming heart
to the envious gods: 'O mortal men
worshipped by the goddesses who gave you a share
of ambrosia on Olympus with their embrace,
o mortals crushed by the envious
gods...' And the divine curse withers
the cool celery and the violets,
and goes on its way, and like hail sent by divine wrath it burns
the grapes on the fruitful vines.
Only the famous hero from Thiaki,
who lit it as a passer-by, is not shaken
by the nymph's flaming-hearted curse.
The shipwrecked, sea-tossed one sits
outside, unshakeable as always, and looks out,

and remembers his homeland, and keeps on weeping
to the shore and the deep, deep seas.
And the white gull which plunges its wings again and again
with momentum into the spray in search of fish,
and the hawk roosting in the wood,
take up, and moan in return to, the strong one's weeping ...
—Oh the first-spied vision of fancy,
oh the uncovering of the beautiful before me!
And look, the swarthy, poor, little town
has turned into the nymph's bright white island;
and look, the humble little girl, the fisher-girl,
is like Calpyso bright-haired, burned by love!
And look, my heart within, traveller to a thousand
places, thirsty for a homeland, love!
And look, ever since, my soul again and again
a two-stringed harp echoing the ancient
harmony, either curse or weeping ...
Divine Homer, joy and glory of the ages![5]

This poem, from a sequence recalling the poet's childhood, revolves around a contrast between the graceless environment in which the poet has to live and the beautiful and stirring world of Homer that is opened up to us by reading. Indeed, the poet shows a sense of isolation from Homer's world that we associate rather with the northern Europeans: take Arnold's peroration to his lecture on translating Homer, where he speaks of 'the pure lines of an Ionian horizon, the liquid clearness of an Ionian sky'.[6] Palamas stresses the alteration, that can only be made through the powerful imagination of a poet such as himself, of a mundane and un-Homeric world: he draws a distinction, in particular, between Homer as a classroom exercise and the sights and sounds that Homer produces in the unfettered poetic mind. (We may compare Pope: '*Homer* makes us Hearers, and *Virgil* leaves us Readers.'[7]) The claim, coming from a modern Greek poet, is that it is possible for a poet's imagination to overleap even the barrier that separates him from Homer. It is

[5] Palamas, «Ραψωδία», Ἅπαντα vol. 3, p. 64–5.
[6] Matthew Arnold, *Essays Literary and Critical* (London 1907), p. 275.
[7] Alexander Pope, *The Iliad of Homer* (2 vols. ed. Maynard Mack *et al.*, London 1967), vol. 1, p. 8.

important to note in this connection that Palamas' first acquaintance with Homer, in 1874, pre-dates the appearance of Polilas' dignified translation of the *Odyssey*.[8] Indeed, when Palamas inserts into his rhapsody on Homer part of an actual 'rhapsody' – the episode from Book 5 of the *Odyssey* – it echoes quite closely Polilas' translation of the passage.[9] Palamas' Homer continues to have a strong Ionian connection, unspoken though it may be in this poem; but the connection perhaps works against the central claim of the poem, that identity with the Homeric world is impossible, and that all that the modern poet can do is provide reflections of it.[10] At any rate, Homer does not become an abiding preoccupation of Palamas – an indication that, although the shade of Homer exercises a fascination for many of the modern Greek poets, we must not see it as looming over the whole of the modern literature. In the case of Palamas we find a preference to turn to parts of the Greek tradition that he can tap more naturally, parts which do not appear to be separated by so abrupt a barrier: the Byzantine 'epic' *Digenes Akrites*; folk song; Solomos and Valaoritis.

But the Homeric poems did provide Palamas with a *persona* from which the poet derived almost as much inspiration over the years as Seferis was to derive from the figure of Odysseus: the bard Phemius. Phemius, we recall, was the bard in residence at the palace of Odysseus who sang for the Suitors under duress during his master's absence, and who alone among the whole crowd was spared when Odysseus found him skulking in the hall after the slaughter. Phemius Terpiades, 'Fame-giver, son of Enjoyment-giver', is seen as being, on the one hand, weaker than other men, and therefore not liable to their fate, and, on the other, as the possessor of a divine gift beyond their attainment. Palamas persistently saw himself as a type of Phemius: small of stature, weedy, not a man of action by contrast with his family tradition; and yet with a gift for expressing himself in verse. In 'Phemius', a poem of 1903, he gives a polemical twist

8 K. G. Kasínis, Ἡ ἑλληνικὴ λογοτεχνικὴ παράδοση στὴ «Φλογέρα τοῦ Βασιλιᾶ» (Athens 1980), p. 168.

9 See especially Polilas, Ἡ Ὀδύσσεια (Athens 1875–81), 5.55–71.

10 Note the phrase τοῦ δυνατοῦ τὸ κλάμα and compare Solomos' τοῦ δυνατοῦ τὴν κλάψα in his poem «Ὁ πόρφυρας», Ἅπαντα vol. 1, p. 255.

to this poetic *persona*, beginning with an epigraph from Polilas' *Odyssey* Book 22:

> The bard Terpiades escaped black fate,
> Phemius, who sang for the suitors under duress.
> 'And I am self-taught, and God has given birth to
> thousands of songs in my heart...'

The poem runs as follows:

> 'I must have angered one of the gods; some great sin
> thrust me here among you;
> I am pure rhythm, you the impure wave
> of the blind and the rabid.
> I, Terpiades, have been thrust by an unjust curse
> to serve a forlorn sentence,
> and a golden-stringed lute mingles its song
> with your howling, wolves.
> Did you dream of me as an obedient mouth, slave
> for your revelling?
> I am no fragile little boat; I do not tremble
> at the headland of your falsehood.
> The king is away abroad and the palace is empty;
> pour in, roisterers!
> Each corner and space of the palace is full
> of Penelope.
> And if you now desire her and lewdly stretch out
> your hands to her,
> the gods are at her side; around her always peace
> and strength from the stars.
> And night and day she fights, weaver and unraveller,
> weaves and unweaves,
> until her husband come, the one creative
> joy for ever that awaits her.
> And the husband will return avenger; he will stretch
> the great bow;
> and all, without mercy, one upon another,
> will give you to the birds.
> And the only obstacle to his bow
> will be the grace of my song;

a king am I too, and the king who will return
  will take me to his side.
Penelope will be encircled by an Olympian brightness,
  as she bends over the loom,
and far and wide, even the narrowest chink will shine
  with resurrecting gleam.
And just as the jackals' yelps beat
  the air around you,
Polymnia's hands will bear me in the air
  towards the azure day!'

Among the rash herd of the wicked,
such things did you see prophetic and reflect on,
hunched over your lyre, o Phemius Terpiades,
and from the night of your pain you moulded songs,
    just as in pitch
there are some colours that shine most brightly.[11]

To pick on Phemius rather than on Homer himself (or perhaps on Demodocus, the bard in the romantic world of the Phaeacians) is an unusual move for a public poet, one that Palamas made his own. It needs to be understood, perhaps more closely than most of the poems discussed in this study, as having a political context: as Registrar of the University of Athens at this time, Palamas became embroiled in controversy, as the debate about the Greek language took to the streets with bloody results. In this poem the poet is denouncing the rotten state of affairs in Greece following the humiliating defeat by the Turks in 1897; and his particular concern is with the climate of intimidation that puts his whole mode of expression in jeopardy.

Palamas' last collection, published in 1935, is entitled *The Nights of Phemius*, and it contains numerous references to Homer and to the bard he created. But, perhaps surprisingly in view of the title, Homeric allusion does not assume great importance in this collection: references to the Homeric poems in particular are hard to pin down. In these little four-line poems, the best of them triumphs of compression, Homer appears in the most diverse company: with

[11] Palamas, Ἅπαντα vol. 3, pp. 188–9.

Kornaros, the Veneto-Cretan Renaissance poet; with Vālmīki; with Shakespeare, Alexander and Newton.[12] One can argue, indeed, that in making Homer part of a world company, Palamas is the most European of Greek poets; and this receives some confirmation from the most relevant section of what is on any account his masterpiece, *The Twelve Lays of the Gipsy*. In this section, entitled 'The Death of the Ancients', Palamas outlines his principle of allusion with a programmatic statement; as part of a long speech to the Ancients, the Gipsy tells them:

> And whoever becomes your slave
> and follows in your train,
> whether an individual or a whole race,
> will be extinguished with you.
> And only he who will not
> lose himself with you,
> and will but pick your flowers
> to crown his hair –
> only he here below
> adorned like a bridegroom will pull ahead,
> will pull ahead adorned with your grace,
> will pull ahead.[13]

Palamas' principle about the ancients is tied up with his belief in Progress: the ancients, even Homer, are, like all past literature, to be used by the modern poet as a quarry of words and themes; they do not form part of a simultaneous order – in Eliot's phrase – in which he must himself live.[14] This principle will, as we shall see, be overturned, in different ways, by the three poets who are the main subject of this book; at any rate, it is characteristic of Palamas at his best that it is out of a sense of isolation from Homer and the ancients that he develops memorable poetry.

[12] Palamas, Ἅπαντα vol. 9, pp. 508, 482, 504.

[13] Palamas, «Ὁ θάνατος τῶν ἀρχαίων», Ἅπαντα vol. 3, p. 352.

[14] Eliot, *Sacred Wood*, p. 49.

PART TWO

SIKELIANOS

*

Chapter Four
The Homeric inheritance

I

Both Solomos and Palamas, as we have seen, pay homage to Homer; Angelos Sikelianos, whose achievement it is to have made himself poetically a successor to both, did the same in a famous poem from his first collection, *Visionary*, 'Homer':

> And it was as if some unseen hand
> rested on my shoulder,
> and I thought I was leading some
> blind man on the night way.
> I could hear in my ear the unwritten,
> deep law of creation.
> And I opened my eyelids
> wide, big,
> lest even one drop
> of the great light be spilt;
> as the olive-trees around me
> in the wood, late at night,
> shone with the secret
> oil that fills them.
>
> And as he went on up,
> staring into the distance,
> like Odysseus I wiped
> the tear from my eyelids.[1]

This poem appears as part of a sustained celebration by the poet of his native land, the island of Lefkáda (Leucas), and it might seem that Homer belongs here through the commonplace that Homer

[1] Angelos Sikelianos, «Όμηρος» (from Ἀλαφροΐσκιωτος) in Λυρικὸς βίος (6 vols. ed. G. P. Savidis, Athens 1965–9), vol. 1, p. 137; on Homeric allusion in the collection as a whole see Ricks, 'Homer and Greek Poetry', pp. 105–21.

and Nature are the same; but the poem is more literary than this. For the tribute to the poetic vocation clearly has Solomos' 'Shade of Homer' behind it.

One important difference between the poems is of course immediately striking: the Shade is not seen but heard. The title of the collection is relevant here: the word for visionary, ἀλαφροΐσκιωτος (literally, 'light-shadowed'), denotes in folk tradition one who has the power to see magical spirits. When explaining the term for a scholarly audience in 1871, the founder of Greek folklore studies, N. G. Polítis (1852–1921), characteristically used a Homeric example:

> This belief is founded on the idea that the human eye, as if with a mist before it, is unable to distinguish supernatural objects. Thus in Homer Athena tells Diomede, 'And I have removed the mist that before was over your eyes so that you may clearly see god and man alike.'[2]

And the word ἀλαφροΐσκιωτος received famous poetic sanction in two lines from the third draft of Solomos' unfinished *magnum opus*, 'The Free Besieged' (1844):

> Good visionary, say what you have seen tonight.
> – A night full of wonders, a night scattered with magic.[3]

The self-proclaimed visionary poet has supernatural powers: the physical appearance of the Shade need not therefore be described. Hence the unseen hand that rests on the younger poet's shoulders, and hence the reworking of a phrase used by Solomos of Ossian in his 'Ode to the Moon': ἀκουμβοῦσε | σὲ μιὰν ἐτιά ('he was leaning on a willow') becomes μοῦ ἀκούμπησε στὸν ὦμο.[4] But we should not interpret the younger poet's guidance of Homer as overweening: the poet is rather in the position of the boy who leads Tiresias.[5]

The lines that follow are not intuitively easy to connect with the foregoing, at any rate if we take the poem in isolation: what we need to be aware of is Sikelianos' persistent preoccupation with

[2] N. G. Politis, Νεοελληνική μυθολογία (Athens 1979), p. 102.
[3] Solomos, Ἅπαντα vol. 1, p. 245.
[4] Solomos, Ἅπαντα vol. 1, p. 57.
[5] *Pace* Savidis, 'Burden of the Past', p. 173.

mountains as the home of poetic inspiration (this he derives from his Leucadian predecessor Valaoritis); and we thus understand why Homer and his heir are taking the path to the sublime. (It may not be too fanciful to relate the gleaming of the oil to a line of Homeric translation that survives in Solomos' remains: πoὺ γλυκoλαμπυρίζει ὡσὰν τὸ λάδι (*Iliad* 18.596, mistranslated: 'and it gives a sweet gleam like oil'). The adjustment whereby a surface gleam is now seen as coming from within the trees would be characteristic of Sikelianos' visionary poetics.[6]) As Homer ascends to the heights, watching the distance only metaphorically, through his poetic vision, the contrast between his physical and his spiritual powers of vision moves his heir to tears; the sense of Homer's power in weakness once again owes something to Solomos' lines from the 'Shade',

> And towards the many stars of the aether
> he rolled his extinguished eyes.

The younger poet compares himself to Odysseus in a recollection of *Odyssey* 19.512, where the hero is moved to tears by his conversation with Penelope, but must conceal them until the task of killing the Suitors is done; Sikelianos has Polilas' rendering in mind:

> στὰ βλέφαρ' ὡς ἀφάνιζε τὰ δάκρυα του
>
> ('*as he wiped the tears from his eyelids*')

But the poet's identification of himself with Odysseus here is not one of boastful bravado: it is an acknowledgement of the primacy of the hero's creator, Homer, and the capacity of his poetry to move us still.

In 'Homer', which was written not so long after Palamas' 'Rhapsody' and immediately in the wake of 'The Death of the Ancients', Sikelianos articulates a sense of intimacy with Homer which Palamas would never have wished to claim; and there is no reason to doubt that in this poem the younger poet has set out, through recourse to Solomos, consciously to surpass the unofficial

6 The line of Homer in Solomos, Ἅπαντα vol. 1, p. 317; on the importance of Solomos for Sikelianos generally see the comment of Savidis in Sikelianos, Λυρικὸς βίος vol. 6, p. 8 and K. Th. Dimaras, Ἱστορία τῆς νεοελληνικῆς λογοτεχνίας (Athens 1985), pp. 242–3.

laureate, Palamas: a comparison with Palamas has indeed much to tell us. In the first instance, we may take the way in which Homer's words in the ear of his guide coincide with an illumination from the natural world; there is a pointed contrast here with a passage from 'The Death of the Ancients' in which the Gipsy declares:

> If ever I find a papyrus,
> I burn it to secure
> heat or light;
> I light my fire indiscriminately,
> in any ruined foundation,
> whether palace or monastery,
> school or church.
>
> And from the flame and the blaze
> all around me birds and trees
> and reptiles
> shine, crackle, quiver, change,
> and the whole of nature becomes spirit
> and whispers secretly to me
> mantic words.[7]

The impulse here is to secure inspiration destructively, in defiance of nature, through an artificial light: through the destruction of what is human the poet achieves natural inspiration. A second point notable in 'Homer' – and related to the first in that it implies the harmony of poetry with the natural world which the poem celebrates – is its formal control: the division of the rhyming couplets (AAABBCCDD) does in itself give an emphasis to the subject-matter; but it also shows an aspiration to exploit possibilities not exploited by Palamas. The Greek rhyming couplet is at its best a strong and supple form, and Sikelianos' couplets here could not have been written without the example of Solomos' dramatic monologue known as 'The Cretan' (1833–4).[8] But the young poet has, in one way, extended the capacities of the form through his lineation: by doubling the number of line-endings he creates opportunities to surprise the reader out of familiarity.

[7] Palamas, Ἅπαντα vol. 3, p. 354.

[8] Solomos, «Ὁ Κρητικός», Ἅπαντα vol. 1, pp. 197–206.

II

Sikelianos' return to Solomos, however, is not to be understood simply as a tribute to the 'Shade' nor as the revival of a neglected form (the phenomenon of 'leapfrogging' mentioned in the Introduction): there are reasons of local patriotism. The sense that their native land had Odyssean connections persisted among the inhabitants of the Ionian Islands. Even in the sixteenth century Homer had figured in a dispute between Cephalonia and Zante, and during a later crisis we can see Homer's political significance, at least:

> When in 1797, after the capture of Venice by the French, General Gentili arrived in Corfu, in the guise of friendship but in reality to capture the Ionian Islands and adorn with them the badge of the French Republic, he included in his announcement, in accordance with the express instructions of Bonaparte, the names of Miltiades and Themistocles. But the archpriest of Corfu... astonished the General and Napoleon himself. 'Frenchmen', he said, 'you will not find in this island a people learned in the letters and sciences for which nations are famed. But do not despise it for that, but learn to estimate it by reading this book here.' And with these words he handed the General the *Odyssey* of Homer.[9]

Sikelianos had articulated with a naive directness the sense that he was heir to both Homer and Solomos in an early uncollected poem, 'The Stranger' (1905):

> 'Stranger, what is your land and what your name?'
>
> 'Even I am still in a dream, I am no stranger;
> I see a blue seashore and olive-trees delicately woven,
> I see too a castle cast on the glass of the open sea.'
>
> 'But in what cove is drawn up the swift boat on which you came?'

[9] For the dispute see K. Th. Dimaras, Νεοελληνικὸς διαφωτισμός (Athens 1977), pp. 131–2; quotation by Andónios Mátesis, «Ὁ Σολωμὸς καὶ ἡ Ζάκυνθος», in Διαλέξεις περὶ Ἑλλήνων ποιητῶν vol. 1 ('Parnassós' Society, Athens 1925), pp. 169–203; quotation on p. 176.

'It is drowned in the island's light. But rather come forward
yourself;
show me where are your gardens, where your golden apples.
And do not speak to me of the bronze dogs of godlike Alcinous;
but detain the garden keeper that I may enter,
and there I shall tell you my name and how I reached this land.
And then, my good girl, show us the sanctified streets
down which Solomos used to go of an evening.'[10]

With this poem, Sikelianos first puts himself on native ground after the foreign influences of his earliest poems: the two proper names alert us to what – even in this embryonic form – is a synthesis of Homer and the modern Greek poetic tradition designed to rival Palamas.[11] The presence of Solomos and Alcinous together indicates that the setting is the familiar Scheria–Corfu, and the poem expatiates neatly on this aspect by working in narrative elements from the part of the *Odyssey* in which the island appears. When Odysseus is shipwrecked on Scheria in Book 6 he encounters the princess Nausicaa, and it is agreed that he will be able to enjoy the hospitality of her parents if he comes to their palace. But the princess fears the wagging tongues of the townsfolk and so asks Odysseus to make his way on his own; Athena, disguised as a small girl, gives Odysseus instructions when she meets him in town; and this is the girl addressed in the second half of Sikelianos' poem, firmly rooted in the original episode through his references to Alcinous' palace and garden (*Odyssey* 7.1–132). The stranger, then, is a sort of Odysseus, and this is developed further by the two questions the girl asks him, which are those asked of Odysseus by the queen, Arete, when he supplicates her (7.332ff.). Through these knowing references to Homer, the speaker of 'The Stranger' declares himself to be no stranger, paving the way for the intimacy the poet will claim in 'Homer'.

In Greek Romantic poetry the notion that the poet may derive inspiration from the mere enduring presence of Homer in the Greek

[10] Sikelianos, Λυρικὸς βίος vol. 6, p. 55.

[11] Solomos' reported preference for the *Odyssey* over the *Iliad* may be relevant here (Ἅπαντα vol. 1, p. 31).

landscape is a persistent one; take the lines of Aleksandros Sutsos:

> and the Zephyr's breeze
> whispers Homer's ancient melody

or those of Aristoménis Proveléngios (1850–1936):

> and in the midst of the charmed sea
> beats in the echo of the rocks,
> sounds still Homer's
> haunted lyre,
> like the whisper of the infinite.[12]

Sikelianos puts flesh on the bones of this fancy, as we have seen, by rooting his poems in the tradition of the Homeric poems themselves; and, in the context of *Visionary* as a whole, 'Homer' takes on a further force through the articulation of a sense of autochthony. This is vigorously made in the fourth poem of *Visionary*, in which is contained only one of a large number of passing echoes of Homer:

> And I said, looking all around,
> 'Island,
> unsetting glory on the sea,
> o rooted in sounding space
> and bathed in Homer's verse,
> sunk in hymn!
>
> Forest all oak on your summit,
> an iron-strung welling-up
> on which my guts, a divine holocaust,
> have steamed;
> and your peak trembles like a leaf;
> inland roars the Lefkatas wind;
> the storm gathers,
> breaks in the divine olive-grove,
> makes tempestuous the sea;
> my island;
> other nurture than my nurture
> I shall never find,
> than my soul no other soul,
> than my body no other body.

[12] Sútsos in Hrístos E. Angelomátis, Ἑλληνικὰ ρωμαντικὰ χρόνια (Athens n.d.), p. 47; Proveléngios in Palamas, Ἅπαντα vol. 12, pp. 287–8.

Elsewhere are the temples, elsewhere the gods.
Around me flashes with lightning the lot of heroes.
You subordinated my solitude to my power.
The grey-eyed one's care is my inheritance![13]

So far we have considered Sikelianos as a native of the islands in general; but in this apostrophe to Lefkada, identified here by the mention of the wind, the poet is claiming a still closer affinity to Homer. For, according to Schliemann's pupil Wilhelm Dörpfeld, whose view Sikelianos was, not surprisingly, eager to believe, modern Lefkada, and not modern Thiaki, was the Homeric Ithaca.[14] These lines are indeed written in the light of Odysseus' declaration that he inhabits the island of Ithaca, 'whose mountain is the great Neritos with its shaking leaves' (*Odyssey* 9.21–2); in harmony with this natural inheritance the poet lays claim also to the protection of the grey-eyed goddess Athena, her epithet taken from Polilas' translation of the *Odyssey*.

All this stress on rootedness stands in the most determined contrast to Palamas' Gipsy, with his denial of native roots; in particular, the continued value of Homer as originator of a tradition defies Palamas' doubts about the ancients. And it is precisely through his adherence to the Ionian Islands' tradition that Sikelianos is able to overcome any such doubts and affirm the place of Homer. The famous last lines of 'The Death of the Ancients' anticipate the conquest of Constantinople in 1453:

the Sultan on horseback
entered, the destroyer.[15]

But the Ionian Islands remained always part of the West, despite a number of close calls, and the Ionian poet's sense of tradition need not involve the mere manuscript transmission that Palamas rejects as lifeless and inadequate. In 'Homer', as in *Visionary* overall, we have an awareness, at least, of the tradition of Solomos; in two poems of his maturity which we shall go on to examine, Sikelianos will give concision and point to poems which draw more self-consciously on Homer.

[13] Sikelianos, «Ὁ βαθὺς λόγος», Λυρικὸς βίος vol. 1, pp. 90–1.

[14] Sikelianos, Πεζὸς λόγος (4 vols. ed. G. P. Savidis, Athens 1978–84), vol. 1, p. 12.

[15] Palamas, Ἅπαντα vol. 3, p. 355.

Chapter Five
Greek romanticism comes of age

I

'When it was a matter of wonder', Landor wrote, 'how Keats, who was ignorant of Greek, could have written his 'Hyperion', Shelley, whom envy never touched, gave as a reason – "because he *was* a Greek".'[1] This dictum raises a question about the poetry discussed in this book: how, given the fact that modern Greece has acquired Homer from the West, is the modern Greek poet to *Hellenize* the relationship between Homer and himself? Archaism and kleftism were inadequate answers; the local patriotism of *Visionary* offered the possibility of a new role for Homer; but there was room for a more literary mode of allusion. A particularly self-conscious possibility was to acknowledge the Western contribution to modern Hellenism, as Sikelianos so generously does in 'Yánnis Keats' (1915):

A bough Apollo's hand;
a plane-tree's smooth, full bough,
spread above you, may it bring
the ambrosial calm of the universe ...

I thought how you would arrive at Pylos' broad, bright shore
    in my company,
with Mentor's tall ship gently moored
    in the sand's embrace;

how we, bound in the winged friendship of those youths
    who fly with the gods,
would go to the stone seats which time
    and the folk had made smooth

in order to meet that man who even in the third generation
    was governing in peace;
whose discourse of travels and holy judgements matured
    in his mind as he grew older ...

[1] In *De Quincey as Critic* (ed. John E. Jordan, London 1973), p. 469.

How we would be there at the sacrifice to the gods, at dawn,
 of the three-year-old heifer,
and hear the single cry uttered by his three daughters
 when the axe roared

and suddenly plunged in darkness
 the slow-rolling, dark-lashed eye,
with the dull gilded half-moon
 of its horns useless...

My love, as a sister a brother,
 imagined your virginal bath,
how Polycaste would bathe you naked
 and clothe you in a beautiful tunic.

I thought how I would awake you at dawn
 with a shove of my foot,
lest we delay while the bright chariot
 yoked awaited us;

and how all day long, in silence or with the simple talk
 that comes and goes,
we would steer the horses which are always tugging the yoke
 to one side or the other...

But most of all I thought how
 your two deer's eyes
would forget themselves over the bronze and the bright gold
 in the palace of Menelaus,

and would gaze unswervingly, burying them in depths
 inaccessible to memory,
at the heavy amber, the gilded and the white ivory,
 the carved silver...

I thought how, bending to your ear, I would tell you in a quiet
 lowered voice:
'Watch out, my friend, because soon Helen will appear
 before our eyes;
before us will appear the Swan's only daughter,
 soon, here before us;
and with that we will sink our eyelids
 in the river of Oblivion.'

*

So brightly you appeared before me; but what grass-covered roads
have brought me to you!
The fiery roses with which I have strewn your tomb
and through which Rome flowers for you

point out to me your pure gold songs – just like
the mighty, armed bodies
which you see intact in a newly-opened ancient tomb, and which vanish
even as you look at them ... –

and all the worthy treasury of Mycenae which I thought
to lay before you –
the cups and swords and broad diadems;
and on your dead beauty

a mask like that which covered
the king of the Achaeans,
pure gold, crafted, hammered out
on the trace of death![2]

The question of East and West raises itself in the very title of 'Yannis Keats', through which Keats becomes an honorary Greek. Why 'Yannis' rather than 'John'? This is not to be seen merely as an orthodox use of the demotic idiom: the rest of the poem does not bear this out. The proposal that this form of the name indicates a special affection for Keats is right; but the really important thing is that the title here makes Keats Greek, and a Greek of the present, bringing him into the Greek world as the more formal 'Ioannes' would not.[3] The poem's epigraph, by contrast, is easily ignored by the reader and not intuitively easy to connect with what follows. Very different in form and idiom from the rest of the poem, it is believed by the poet's editor to be a piece of juvenilia. Written, it seems, before the poet was twenty, the lines look like an attempt to imitate Keats: note the presence of Apollo, a favoured deity.[4] These

[2] Sikelianos, «Γιάννης Κῆτς», Λυρικὸς βίος vol. 2, pp. 127–9; but I punctuate according to the first publication in Γράμματα 3 (1915), 5–7.

[3] On this point, and generally, see G. P. Savidis, «Ὁ Σικελιανὸς καὶ οἱ Ἄγγλοι ποιητές», Νέα Ἑστία no. 1307 (Christmas 1984), 92–103.

[4] *A Concordance to the Poems of John Keats* (ed. M. G. Becker *et al.*, New York and London 1981).

elements in the epigraph evidently run counter to the demands of the nationalist art critic, Periklís Yannópulos (1869–1910), a figure who exerted a strong influence on the young Sikelianos: in 1902 he urged the Greeks

> to recreate in a new spirit our entire Mythological World, imagining as we wish the Aphrodites and Adonises, giving expression as we wish to our nymphs and satyrs, but with our own aesthetic of shape and colour, so as to counterpose them to the corresponding European works.[5]

But Sikelianos is a poet, not a nationalist ideologue, and he is in this poem trying to effect a *rapprochement* between Western Hellenism and 'the real thing'. By recalling in the epigraph, no doubt out of some original context, the lines he wrote as a youth under the influence of Keats, Sikelianos acknowledges an early poetic love (as he explains in a lecture of 1947) but also shows how his idiom has developed in the intervening years: he pays tribute to Keats in diction now less obtrusively literary.[6] But 'Yannis Keats' is literary in a broader sense. The poem is not merely a sort of belated Greek *Adonais* based on a legendary Keats as spiritual presence: it is an act of homage to the poet that the Greek and the European hold in common – Homer.

The question of course arises: is Homer held in common? Keats' 'Chapman's Homer' naturally springs to mind. But it is another poem by Keats, whether or not Sikelianos himself read it, that offers us another way into 'Yannis Keats': 'To Homer' begins,

> Standing aloof in giant ignorance,
> Of thee I hear and of the Cyclades,
> As one who sits ashore and longs perchance
> To visit dolphin-coral in deep seas.[7]

Unlike Byron, of course, Keats neither knew Greek nor ever visited Greece. In addressing a poem to Keats, then, and in doing so through allusion to Homer, Sikelianos is seeking to bring the spiritually Grecian poet into the actual Greek world of literature and life.

[5] Periklís Yannópulos, Ἡ ἑλληνική γραμμή (Athens 1965), p. 65; Sikelianos' poem on him in Λυρικὸς βίος vol. 2, pp. 63–7.

[6] Sikelianos, «Γιάννης Κῆτς», Ἀγγλοελληνική Ἐπιθεώρηση 2 (1947), 345–50.

[7] John Keats, *Poems* (Oxford 1972), p. 366.

II

'Yannis Keats' is divided by typography into two parts. The first recreates a Homeric world in which the kindred spirits of Keats and his Greek admirer are imagined to meet: it does so by drawing openly on the *Odyssey*. As a citizen of Homer's world – politically, and, as he will have to prove through the poem, poetically – Sikelianos extends to the Englishman an invitation to visit it, no longer just 'looking into Chapman's Homer' – a mere book – but with a view of that world as seen by a Greek with his own eyes. (The impressions were in fact fresh in the poet's mind because he had recently made a grand tour of the ancient and medieval sites of Greece in the company of Kazantzakis.) Together with the second part, the tribute paid to Keats by the poem is that he is, in Cavafy's phrase, 'that finest thing, Hellenic'.[8]

By setting out to recreate a Homeric world, Sikelianos may seem to have imposed on himself a hard task, risking being swallowed up by Homer. And, as any reader of Homer can see – the poem is as clear a case as any discussed in this book – the first part of 'Yannis Keats' is a selective but undisguised rehearsal of the Telemachy, beginning in Book 3 of the *Odyssey*. But this part of the *Odyssey* is not chosen just for its picturesque detail, and the decision to make the first part of 'Yannis Keats' a Telemachy rather than an Odyssey is not a casual one. Now it is true that, whereas Odysseus is a mythical figure with an acknowledged existence outside the *Odyssey*, Telemachus has no fleshed-out independent existence: he exists only insofar as we read the *Odyssey* as a poem as opposed to raw myth. With Homer's stamp so clearly on him, Telemachus looks like a figure little susceptible of revival – but Sikelianos' treatment of Telemachus is not without sophistication and point.

While it appears on a casual reading that the narrative of the Telemachy is simply reproduced in 'Yannis Keats' – so many of the familiar Homeric details find their way into the later poem – this is not in fact the case. It is true that Sikelianos' poem is clearly rooted in the Telemachy in the translation of Polilas, even to the placing of

[8] Cavafy, «'Επιτύμβιον 'Αντιόχου, βασιλέως Κομμαγηνῆς», Ποιήματα vol. 2, p. 36.

words in the lines.[9] But we have in the first place a formal adjustment which enables the poet to recreate in a lyric mode, without redundancy, the following Homeric line (*Odyssey* 3.486) as a whole stanza:

> and all day they swung the yoke, holding it on either side.

Furthermore, the speaker of the poem imagines himself and Keats into a Homeric world without the identities of either being fully subsumed within the Homeric figures; working back from the end of the first part of the poem is, oddly, the best way to illustrate this. The poet whispers to Keats at the same juncture as Telemachus whispers to Pisistratus (*Odyssey* 4.71); but the actual words uttered by Telemachus in the epic are those broadly reproduced by Sikelianos just before as the subject of Keats' attention. Earlier, we find Sikelianos assuming the role of Telemachus (*Odyssey* 15.45) in waking Pisistratus; but in the lines that precede, it is Keats, like Telemachus in the *Odyssey* (3.464–8), who is being bathed by Polycaste. For the four preceding stanzas, finally, all actions are shared and all verbs plural, returning us to the starting-point, at which Sikelianos and Keats arrive together at Pylos – with the consequence that neither can be identified with Pisistratus, who is already there. In the light of these blendings of the Homeric roles, the phrase 'as a sister a brother' completes the affinity of the two poets, making it clear that, although 'Yannis Keats' sets out to bring Keats into a Homeric world he has never known, it brings him in on equal terms, not with a suggestion that, as a foreigner, he is lucky to be there.

Sikelianos thus draws on the Telemachy without reproducing it, overturning it or deriving a moral from it; and he exploits the fact that a Telemachy detached from the body of the *Odyssey* is a very particular sort of thing, a subject offering limited but real poetic possibilities. If we detach the Telemachy from the epic as a whole its place as a foil to the return journey of Odysseus disappears, as do the darker shadows cast by the narrations of Nestor and Menelaus. What is left is a rite of passage, without the responsibility to seek the father

[9] Polilas, Ὀδύσσεια 3.449–50, 464–8; 4.69–75.

(*Odyssey* 2.215), through a world that is all beauty and optimism. We thus find in 'Yannis Keats' that all the experiences are dwelt on for their value as experience: the cry of Nestor's daughters in the *Odyssey*, for example, is a human touch, to be sure, but it does not appear in as high relief there as it does in 'Yannis Keats'. The value of experience for its own sake is not of course alien to the Telemachy, but it is subordinate to a larger whole. In 'Yannis Keats', by contrast, we find a point of affinity with Cavafy's 'Ithaca', published in the same magazine four years earlier: we may settle on the line

> the heavy amber, the gilded and the white ivory

and compare it to Cavafy's

> pearl and coral, amber and ebony.[10]

The feature of the Telemachy as experience which brings 'Yannis Keats' to a close is Helen.

Up to this point all the chosen episodes of the *Odyssey* have been told without substantial alteration: the arrival at Pylos, the meeting with Nestor, the sacrifice, the bath, the journey to Sparta, the effect on the young visitors of the palace's splendour, the speech of the one to the other; but now there is a difference which takes this new poem decisively away from Homer. In Homer, the subject of this conversation is not Helen – the poet, as often, resists the temptation to produce a description – and when Helen does appear no reference is made to her supernatural origins. (The sole mention of these in Homer is *Iliad* 3.418: 'born of Zeus'.) For Sikelianos, by contrast, the beauty of Helen is the culmination of any journey in the world of Homer – but the strength of this part of the poem is that the prediction of Helen's appearance is left at that, and this owes something to Keats as well as to Homer. For Sikelianos and Keats his guest the anticipated sight of Helen brings forgetfulness of the troubles of this world, just as the Helen of the *Odyssey* produces the drug *nepenthe* for her guests 'which brings forgetfulness of all evils' (4.221). But the 'river of oblivion' in a poem to Keats will inevitably recall also the 'Ode to a Nightingale', to which the metaphor of

[10] Cavafy, « Ἰθάκη », Ποιήματα vol. 1, pp. 23–4; previously in Γράμματα (Oct.–Nov. 1911).

Sikelianos' second stanza is itself indebted.[11] The celebration of youth through the first part of 'Yannis Keats', culminating in the mention of Helen, is the fulfilment of the poet's wish to forget this world,

> Where Beauty cannot keep her lustrous eyes
> Or new Love pine at them beyond tomorrow.

In the first part of 'Yannis Keats', as we have seen, those very elements which create a Homeric familiarity are subtly altered: Sikelianos' Homeric world is in fact a recreation, not a copy. And Keats is not just superimposed on this Greek world, and is not just a symbol for the Poet, but is woven in: that is, elements from his work are woven in. This process goes a stage further than what we have seen above, as is indeed appropriate if we are to see the comradeship which the poem celebrates as borne out in poetic practice; if we are to see Keats as more than a tourist in the Greek world. Let us look at the stanzas about Nestor. The constituents evidently derive from the description of Nestor in the *Odyssey* (3.244–5); but the adverb 'peacefully' and the adjective 'holy' are not in the Homeric text. Their presence, and the special presence in this Telemachy of the sacrifice at Pylos, are illuminated by a passage from the 'Ode on a Grecian Urn':

> Who are these coming to the sacrifice?
> To what green altar, O mysterious priest,
> Lead'st thou that heifer lowing at the skies,
> And all her silken flanks with garlands drest?
> What little town by river or sea shore,
> Or mountain-built with peaceful citadel,
> Is emptied of this folk, this pious morn?
> And, little town, thy streets for evermore
> Will silent be; and not a soul to tell
> Why thou art desolate, can e'er return.

Note 'peaceful' and 'pious' here: Sikelianos' invitation to Keats to enter a Homeric world is once again seen as connected with Keats' poems.

[11] Sikelianos had a particular affection for this ode: see his lecture «Γιάννης Κῆτς», pp. 345–6.

III

As a tribute to Keats, the first part of 'Yannis Keats' could stand on its own: this part of the poem has bound not only a description of Keats (in the tenth stanza) but also elements from his poetry into a Homeric context in such a way as to answer 'On First Looking into Chapman's Homer'. But 'Yannis Keats' has a second part, separate from, and reflecting against, the first. In this part, the poet, coming to reflect on his reverie, pays open tribute to Keats' poems as having outlasted his lifetime. The roses that he brings to Keats' tomb – and it appears that this is strictly biographical – are as ephemeral as anything in nature, as perishable as the bodies in a newly opened ancient tomb; but they serve to draw our attention to the poems' golden art, the 'pure gold' art as enduring as the 'pure gold' artefacts of Mycenae. The emphasis on the mask as a death mask – more enduring than, but also incompatible with, life – thus reflects back on Keats' poems, with the suggestion that they too were won at the price of life. Keats' youth has been stressed at the beginning of the poem, but his early death, an easy subject to muff, is alluded to only here.

The first part of 'Yannis Keats' evokes a Homeric world of the reading imagination, like that known by Keats through Chapman but more firmly rooted in Greece: the Homeric detail of waking one's companion with a kick (*Odyssey* 15.45) is not one that can be imagined to appear in the Western poetry of Hellenism.[12] Above all, it is since Keats' time that the physical existence of a 'Homeric' world has been confirmed by archaeology in Pylos, Sparta and Mycenae; and the end of 'Yannis Keats' is clearly influenced by Schliemann's claim to have looked upon the face of Agamemnon. It is out of Art, through the imagination, that we fashion a living Homeric world: the conclusion of 'Yannis Keats' is easily related to the 'Grecian Urn'. That is another subject: what we shall have to dwell on at a later point is the way in which, a generation later, Seferis will rewrite 'Yannis Keats', working it into a far more ambivalent response to the enduring presence of Homer's poetry.

[12] Kakridis, *Homer Revisited*, pp. 195–9. Polilas is more genteel: μὲ τὸ πόδι του κινῶντάς τον.

For 'Yannis Keats' is as much a tribute to Homer as to Keats. 'The Stranger' took an easy option by mentioning ancient and modern, Homer and Solomos, together; 'Homer' more subtly alluded to and adjusted Solomos; 'Yannis Keats' honours Homer only by implication. The apparition here is Keats', not Homer's; and it is a strength of 'Yannis Keats' that it does not mention Homer at all, in a recognition that tact can be an asset for the post-Homeric, and especially the modern Greek, poet.

Chapter Six
Beyond Homer

I

'Achelous', another poem of 1915, exhibits on a smaller scale the form of 'Yannis Keats', both metrically and in its two-part structure: a part drawing extensively on Homer, but with important modifications, is followed by a second part reflecting on, and against, the first.

ACHELOUS

(DREAM)

The Aspropotamos was aflood, and I, standing amid
    its terrible impetus,
set down my feet and my upright body above as a pillar,
    like a god resisted...

And suddenly my struggle became a thirst the like of which
                                        was never known;
    and as I opened my lips
to bend down a little and drink, the river
    in unceasing flow rolled into my heart.

And the lighter my heart grew, the sweeter I felt
    the struggle in my limbs,
and I drank like the dawn breeze the current which earlier
    had been beating at my knee.

At last, as foam disappears on a spread of sand
    as a wave goes back,
the river-bed was left quite dry and my feet free,
    wing-like, for me to run!

And thus it was with my relief I felt a boundless virility
    awake in my breast,
and all nature's cool and the mountains' spirit
    was poured into my insides...

*

Oh how much mightier was my dream than the labour
of the demi-god who had seized
the river, in the form of a bull, by the horns,
watching for his opportunity,

and, laying his knee on its thick neck,
broke one of its horns;
and the river poured, mad with pain, into the deep seas,
roaring the while...[1]

The first part of 'Achelous' has a close affinity with an episode in the *Iliad* (21.232–382), as translated into a vigorous demotic by Alexander Pallis (1904).[2] The following lines from this episode, the battle between the avenging Achilles and the river-god Scamander, are particularly relevant (it is noteworthy that the forty-odd lines that Pallis omits from his translation as being an interpolation play no role in Sikelianos' poem):

So he spoke, and aroused anger in the river's guts.
And just when the spear-glorying son of Peleus leapt down
from the steep bank into the middle, at that moment the river
rushes with swollen wave, awaking every stream,
and boiled and thrust forth many corpses, which were floating
in numbers in its waters, slaughtered by the son of Peleus.
It vomited them all out with roaring like a bull
and made its wave boil upright, terrible, all around
Achilles, and fell on his shield and thrust against it, and he could not
stand on his feet. But in the end he embraces
a thick-trunked, tall elm, which comes away at its roots,
and with its fall takes the bank with it, and blocks
the foaming-waved waters with its dense branches.
Then he leaps out from the waves and with winged foot
takes to the plain impetuously, as with the speed
of the night eagle, the hunting eagle,
which is the swiftest of birds, the boldest bird of prey;
even so he ran over the plain...

[1] Sikelianos, «'Αχελῶος», Λυρικὸς βίος vol. 2, pp. 136–7.

[2] Aleksandros Pallis, 'Η 'Ιλιάδα μεταφρασμένη (Paris 1904), 21.232–54, 305–7, 327, 342–5, 381–2.

> but Scamander did not set aside his rabid rage, but was even more
> overcome with anger, and with a harsh upright wave
> rushed on, and kept on pushing him to fall onto his back...

Eventually Hephaestus intervenes on Achilles' behalf, blowing flame on the river, and Scamander yields: 'and all the plain around was dried up, and the foam-clad wave comes to a stop | ... | and the waters run back again into the river-bed'.

It is clear that Sikelianos has adapted the story, and we need to see how. The first modification, that of the river's name, appears in the very first line – but this feature we shall examine shortly. Related to this, however, is the omission, not only of Achilles' name (similar in sound to the river's name), but of the whole context of the Trojan War. The episode has been pruned by Sikelianos of all persons but the narrator, whether they be human (the corpses that clog the river) or divine (the gods who intervene on Achilles' behalf); and what is left is the primeval confrontation of the hero with the elements: note, especially, the absence of the Shield of Achilles as a mark of civilization. The *Iliad* has been adapted here so as to make the hero completely self-reliant: indeed it is the narrator who is put in the position of the angered god. It is for this reason that we find a means of conquering the river appropriate to an Achilles rather than a Hephaestus: to drink the river to the dregs and to let its water (a pervasive metaphor for inspiration in Sikelianos' poetry) flow into his heart. In this connection, we find one reason for the choice of the Aspropotamos: over and above its descriptive name, 'white river', this river is associated with heroism: the Achelous is mentioned in Solomos' 'Hymn to Liberty' (stanza 105) as having been filled with corpses after the first siege of Missolonghi in 1822.

What the modern poet has done, then, is to take a scene from the *Iliad* whose origins lie in old myths of cosmic scope and to turn it back again into a battle of divine forces; and the fourth stanza contains a particular inversion of the epic's narrative which points us to the title of the new poem. Achilles' fleetness of foot is, in the original episode, mentioned in the context of his frightened flight from the river – the one who can defeat all men cannot defeat a god

– and just before his prayer for help: here the winged feet are the sign of triumph over the river. But the distancing of the new poem from the *Iliad* does not end here. In the original episode the height of the conflict is the drying up of the river by Hephaestus, and the resolution of the struggle is marked by the flowing of the waters once again: in 'Achelous' the elemental struggle is to continue in the hero's heart. And the comparison can be made more specific: the river in 'Achelous' is left dry, but the foam which was on the river in the *Iliad* episode has been removed, by a simile, to the waves of the sea. This widening of perspective from river to sea fits the theme of elemental struggle but also constitutes a play on Aspropotamos as a particular river and its alternative name 'Achelous' with its extended sense 'water'.

So far 'Achelous' looks like a condensation of themes from *Visionary* into a smaller compass and a tighter metrical form: it features a super-heroizing of the self by recourse to Homer and it is set in the same Greek world, with the river's twin names rich in associations. But the second part of the poem of course makes it clear that the poet is trading at once on the heroism of the dream and on its status as a dream, claiming for himself not actual heroism but the gift of inspiration through which heroism can be understood. In consequence, the allusiveness of the subtitle is appropriate, ΟΝΕΙΡΟΣ being, not spoken ὄνειρο, but Homeric, as in the phrase 'a divinely sent dream (ὄνειρος) came to me in my sleep'.[3] The content of the dream is, as we have seen, Homeric, with the transformation of memories from Homeric reading being itself dreamlike; but the second half of 'Achelous' takes up a theme pushed to the margins by Homer, the exploits of Heracles (the story is not actually one of the Twelve Labours). Deianeira relates the story in Sophocles' *Trachiniae* (9–21):

> For a river was my suitor, that is Achelous,
> who was asking my father for my hand, in three shapes:
> appearing plainly as a bull; at other times as a flashing,
> curling snake; sometimes with an ox's prow
> on a human trunk, and from his shaggy beard

[3] Theódoros Ksídis, Ἄγγελος Σικελιανός (Athens 1973), pp. 97–9.

flowed down springs of river water.
In the expectation of such a one as my suitor
I was wretched and prayed continually for death
before I should ever come near a bed such as this.
But later on, to my delight,
the glorious son of Zeus and Alcmena came,
and he, coming together in combat with the other one,
set me free.

In Ovid's *Metamorphoses* Achelous himself takes up the story:

Then thirdly did remayne the shape of Bull, and quickly tho
I turning too the shape of Bull rebelld against my fo.
He stepping too my left side cloce, did fold his arms about
My wattled necke, and following mee then running maynely out
Did drag mee backe, and made mee pitch my hornes against the ground,
And in the deepest of the sand he overthrew mee round.
And yit not so content, such hold his cruell hand did take
Upon my welked horne, that he asunder quight it brake,
And pulld it from my maymed brew.[4]

Heracles defeats the river only in the simple form of a bull, and he defeats it only by mutilating it: the narrator of 'Achelous' defeats the element Water by absorbing it into himself. To put the two contests in yet sharper contrast, to the detriment of the former, the modern poet has removed the Homeric source's bull-simile from the first part of 'Achelous' and produced the bull-myth in its full form in the second. The simile, conspicuous by its absence from the first part of 'Achelous', is evidently based on an ancient type of myth of which the combat of Achelous and Heracles is only one example: the scholiast on *Iliad* 21.237 seems to have things topsy-turvy when he writes that 'It is from this point that the post-Homeric poets describe rivers as being in the shape of a bull.'[5] 'Achelous' presupposes the heroic poetry of Homer, yet looks behind this poetry to myth, and then pits this archetype against the yet more heroic voice of the speaker – all in a few lines. There is a

[4] *Shakespeare's Ovid, being Arthur Golding's Translation of the Metamorphoses* (ed. W. H. D. Rouse, London 1961), pp. 183–4.

[5] H. Erbse (ed.), *Scholia Graeca in Homeri Iliadem*, 7 vols. (Berlin 1969–88), on 21.237.

case for hating the search for archetypes – especially in Sikelianos' prose. But here there is some poetic immediacy and purpose to the way in which 'Achelous' exploits a tension between an archetype and its literary development. Homeric allusion in this poem gives concreteness and point to an emotion of poetic power which Sikelianos could not always express so well.

II

Like Cavafy, as we shall see, Sikelianos was never consistently preoccupied with trying to make Homer part of his poetry, and in his later work the significance of Homer dwindles away. In particular the clarity of vision of the Homeric poems becomes for Sikelianos a deficiency, as he seeks to probe the obscurer texts of the ancients, and in particular those of Orphism: though we have in his later work passing references to myths which happen to occur in Homer, the figure of Homer is no longer important. 'Achelous' is evidently one stage on the road to supposed emancipation from Homer; 'Secret Iliad', another poem published in 1915, gives us an idea of how, for good or ill, Sikelianos will turn away from Homer. The poem, which at 201 lines is too long to quote here, describes the apparition of Achilles returning to encourage an effete present day to martial exploits (Greece was about to enter the First World War); its opening lines give an idea of its turbulent idiom:

> O heat of my vigilance,
> unsleeping secret Iliad!
>
> O Hero's thirst,
> robes swift
> as shadows of spring clouds
> before a mountain
> over his cool heart;
>
> calm unthinking
> like a poplar swaying in the breeze from land
> with its root in the spring;

rage sweeter
than scented torch-smoke
in outside air,
in his deep inhalation![6]

This poetic celebration of Greek irredentism has much in common with that of the tract *All Those Alive* by the diplomat and ideologue, Íon Dragúmis (1878–1920); and the centrality of Achilles (though he is not actually named) is not surprising: Greek nationalists set Achilles with Alexander the Great and the legendary lord of the Byzantine Eastern border, Digenes Akrites, as a sort of apostolic succession of national heroes.[7] But Sikelianos in 'Secret Iliad' takes a step beyond his early roots in not just making Achilles his hero but at the same time rejecting altogether the figure of Odysseus, with whom he had been happy to identify himself in 'Homer'. Here Odysseus' ambivalent cunning is rejected in favour of the straightforward physical force of Achilles: recall Achilles' veiled statement of threat to Odysseus at *Iliad* 9.312–13 that

he is as hateful to me as the gates of Hades
who hides one thing in his mind and says another.

The above observations about 'Secret Iliad''s relation to Homer are merely thematic; but the poem's interest is not least in the way in which Homeric allusion is superseded. The long work from which it comes, *Prologue to Life*, is the first extended work of Greek poetry to be written in free verse; and, although there are fine things here, free verse does not, on the whole, bring out the best in Sikelianos. Too often the looseness of the form leads to looseness of thought; exclamations cannot of themselves have the power to revive a hero; we miss the rise and fall of the rhythm in the stanzas of 'Yannis Keats', a delicate handling of the modern Greek poet's coexisting aspirations and restraint in relation to Homer – above all, free verse takes Sikelianos away from his roots, and to Pindar as his model. Two problems immediately spring to mind – or rather one problem

[6] Sikelianos, «Κρυφὴ Ἰλιάδα», Λυρικὸς βίος vol. 3, pp. 89–97, lines 1–14.

[7] Íon Dragúmis, Ὅσοι ζωντανοί (Athens 1911); N. G. Politis, Ἐκλογαὶ ἀπὸ τὰ τραγούδια τοῦ ἑλληνικοῦ λαοῦ (Athens 1969), p. 79.

with poetic and political dimensions. Pindar's genre is uniquely associated with peculiar circumstances of composition and a peculiar role for the poet to which in the modern Greek age Palamas comes closest with his ode for the Olympic Games of 1896: the Pindaric poet cannot be self-appointed.[8] Furthermore, the modern Greek poet reads Pindar as, and will hence rewrite him as, free verse: the risks for a prolix poet like Sikelianos are great.[9]

But what, specifically, are the Pindaric elements in 'Secret Iliad' that diverge from Homer and pull the new poem away from Homer? The hero's special connection with thunder and lightning (lines 147–66) goes back to Pindar, *Pythian* 6.21–5:

> what they say once on a time the son of Philyra [Chiron]
> in the mountains advised the mighty orphan
> son of Peleus; to honour above all
> the gods the son of Cronos, the deep-voiced master
> of lightning and thunder.

Again the supernatural hunting abilities celebrated in lines 79–95 go back to *Nemean* 3.51–2:

> slaying deer without hounds or tricky nets;
> for he excelled in fleetness of foot.

These elements, we note – and whether or not Sikelianos consciously thought this out, there is significance in his being drawn to them – are precisely those of the sort purged by Homer from the Achilles of the *Iliad* in order to make him, except at one or two high points in the action, a human rather than a superhuman figure. It is no cause for surprise, then, that while giving his poem on Achilles the title 'Secret Iliad', Sikelianos draws it away from the Homeric poems, which, too vividly recalled by the reader, might make less convincing the extravagant heroism espoused. Indeed, the only patent reference to the Homeric texts in this poem, a new *Achilleis*, is one of defiant rejection:

> Hero seeking blood
>
> fleeing Hades in thirst

[8] Palamas, Ἅπαντα vol. 5, pp. 319–21.

[9] A modern Greek view of Pindar: Daniíl I. Iakóv, Ἡ ἀρχαιογνωσία τοῦ Ὀδυσσέα Ἐλύτη (Athens 1982), p. 77; on Sikelianos' free verse see Savidis, Πάνω νερά, p. 69.

with Apollo's crow behind you,
gasping, crowing
for you to go back among the Shades!

Oh what could it add to your pure rage and virginity,
the blood that poured from the pied ram
into the trench
when Odysseus went down into Hades
to make question of the dead?[10]

As we shall see, Seferis makes the episode of the *Nekyia* in the *Odyssey* the centre of his whole poetic relationship with Homer: here Sikelianos is in effect denying that the process of retrieval from Homer's poetry has anything to offer him. It is a gesture like Whitman's when he cries,

Come Muse migrate from Greece and Ionia.
Cross out please those immensely overpaid accounts,
That matter of Troy and Achilles' wrath and Aeneas',
Odysseus' wanderings...

– and this example is not taken at random, for Whitman undoubtedly lies behind this vein in the poetry of Sikelianos.[11] At any rate, this poem stands in stark contrast with the explicit point of 'Homer' and the implicit point of 'Yannis Keats', both of which are purposefully allusive to the Homeric poems: in 'Secret Iliad' the connection with Homer has been all but severed, and the *Iliad* becomes, as the title suggests, a physical quality separable from mere words.

[10] Sikelianos, Λυρικὸς βίος vol. 3, pp. 96–7.
[11] Walt Whitman, 'Song of the Exposition', *The Complete Poems* (ed. Frank Murphy, Harmondsworth 1975), p. 226; see Sikelianos, Πεζὸς λόγος vol. 3, pp. 127–9 and P. Prevelákis, Ἄγγελος Σικελιανός (Athens 1984), p. 207.

PART THREE

CAVAFY

*

Chapter Seven
Modes of misquotation

'Homer's world was another matter: it is not strange that he understood quite early on that he must leave it behind.' Seferis' statement about Cavafy's relationship with Homer is probably one of the less disputed claims that the younger poet made about his senior, and it has not been made the subject of a detailed examination.[1] Can we speak of a 'Homeric world' with reference to Cavafy as we undoubtedly can in the case of the early Sikelianos? For the rhetoric of autochthony is alien to Cavafy: outside the Greek state, and initially peripheral, as reader no less than as writer, to its modern literature, he has not the spirit of Homer on which to draw but the letter. (Because of Cavafy's relative isolation from earlier poetic developments in Greece and their implications for Homer, indeed, he appears here after Sikelianos in defiance of their dates of birth; it is to be noted, however, that Cavafy continues to revise one of his poems on Homeric themes, 'The Funeral of Sarpedon', as late as 1924, while the latest of the relevant poems of Sikelianos dates from 1915.)

Yánnis Dállas has remarked of the Greek Romantic period that it

> remembered the ancestral deposits, the Byzantine and above all the ancient. It is to its credit. Its mistake was that it remembered them more or less as a foreigner – that is, like the nations of Europe – and without their substantial assimilation of them and returns gained from them.[2]

[1] Seferis, Δοκιμές vol. 1, p. 400; though a later generation has challenged his assumptions, Seferis' comments are still fundamental. There is a stimulating general survey by D. N. Maronitis, «Κ. Π. Καβάφης: ἕνας ποιητὴς ἀναγνώστης» in Κύκλος Καβάφη (Βιβλιοθήκη Γενικῆς Παιδείας, Athens 1984), pp. 53–80.

[2] Yánnis Dállas, Ἐποπτεῖες Α΄ (Athens 1954), p. 27.

The element of doubt this introduces about the modern Greek poet's relation to the ancients has worried students of Cavafy: one writes defensively that, 'I believe that the ancient-myth poems of Cavafy are composed not only with the mediation of a translation but after careful reading of the original too.'[3] But we need to shelve the assumption that Cavafy read Homer, as it were, cover to cover in the original if we are to look at the relevant poems afresh.

This applies particularly to 'Ithaca', the most famous of all Cavafy's poems, and to 'Trojans', another favourite of anthologists.[4] We have already seen that 'Ithaca' appears to leave a trace in Sikelianos' 'Yannis Keats'; but neither 'Ithaca' nor 'Trojans' is of direct relevance to this study. It is easy to see that both poems are of a different kind from the 'Ancient Days' poems that will be discussed later: both have been described as 'metaphorical'; for neither does the existence of the *Iliad* and the *Odyssey as poems*, or the figure of Homer, have the slightest significance.[5] Each mythical *exemplum* simply *is* the moral of each poem; each has been apprehended in what is perceived to be its essence rather than in any Homeric context. (The fact will disappoint some of the poet's exegetes.[6]) 'Trojans' is about a universal dilemma, not about particular persons; in the case of 'Ithaca', it seems a reasonable assumption that the poem is a later version of the lost 'Second Odyssey' (which was probably written in 1894, the same year as Cavafy's essay, 'The End of Odysseus'): 'Ithaca', itself now proverbial, is about what is called an Odyssey rather than the *Odyssey*.[7] In both cases we are dealing with a subject much broader than that of this book: not the Homeric poems and self-conscious allusion to them, but Homeric myths and their continuing currency. For 'Trojans' refers in general terms to the dilemma of Hector rather than to the events of Books 18–22 of the *Iliad*; 'Ithaca' to the story of Odysseus rather than to the *Odyssey* itself, let alone to Odysseus' narrations in

[3] Maronitis, «Τὰ καβαφικὰ '"Αλογα τοῦ 'Αχιλλέως'», Χάρτης no. 9 (1983), 361–77; quotation from p. 363, n. 6.

[4] Cavafy, «'Ιθάκη», «Τρῶες», Ποιήματα vol. 1, pp. 23–4, 26.

[5] Maronitis, «Κ. Π. Καβάφης», p. 172.

[6] See e.g. I. M. Panayotópulos, Τὰ πρόσωπα καὶ τὰ κείμενα vol. 4 (Athens 1982), pp. 134–6.

[7] Cavafy, «Τὸ τέλος τοῦ 'Οδυσσέως» (ed. G. P. Savidis), Δοκιμασία 2 (1974), 9–22.

it.[8] The hunt for other literary sources, in the case of 'Ithaca' at least, seems to be a never-ending one – Epicurus, Petronius, Dante, Du Bellay, Baudelaire, Tennyson – but traces of the *Odyssey* are only speculatively found.[9]

It is clear from Cavafy's essay on Odysseus, however, that 'Ithaca' has behind it, in the first instance, Tennyson's 'Ulysses'; and it is in general hard to detach Cavafy's Homer from the Victorians. From childhood Cavafy was familiar with the English language; but he was also rather more familiar with English poetry than with Greek poetry, ancient or modern. For the Victorian at its worst we may take the title (probably of 1884), Οἷα [*sic*] περ φύλλων Γενεὴ [*sic*] ('Even as the generation of the leaves').[10] The famous Homeric phrase about the brevity of human life (*Iliad* 6.146) was merely the title, it seems, and was not worked into the body of the poem, if we may judge by a later version of the poem. The phrase has been taken simply as a proverb over which the poet can indulge his mawkish streak: a Turkish proverb would do just as well as an ancient Greek one, and indeed replaces it in the later version.[11] The cliché at which we saw Tennyson poking fun half a century before is now sitting comfortably in that genre of cliché *par excellence*, album verses – and it is pretty plainly of Victorian rather than strictly Homeric provenance.[12] More significantly, it has been placed in a context which perverts the subject of the Homeric passage from death to ageing: the original in Homer, like its parallel in Ecclesiastes ('Even as the green leaves on a thick tree...') has as much to do with the enduring presence of the tree as with the transitoriness of the leaves. In refusing to see the tree for the leaves Cavafy is (no doubt unwittingly) reviving a cheeky subversion of the Homeric passage by the archaic poet Mimnermus, who characteristically treats erotic themes in Homeric diction:

[8] *Pace* Maronitis, «Κ. Π. Καβάφης», pp. 66–7.

[9] For a possible allusion to the *Odyssey* see Ricks, 'Homer and Greek Poetry', pp. 98–100.

[10] Cavafy, Ἀνέκδοτα ποιήματα, p. 6.

[11] Cavafy, Τὰ ἀποκηρυγμένα. Ποιήματα καὶ μεταφράσεις (1886–1896) (ed. G. P. Savidis, Athens 1983), p. 103.

[12] I suspect Pater, *Marius the Epicurean* (London 1924), pp. 152–3, where the Homeric saying appears *apud* Marcus Aurelius 10.34.

We, like the leaves which the flowery season of spring
  brings forth, when they grow swiftly with the sun's rays;
like them, in the flower of our youth for but a short time
  do we enjoy ourselves.[13]

Finally, Cavafy has of course misquoted the Homeric οἵη as οἵα, revealing his ignorance of Homeric Greek.

This combination of types of misquotation we find once again in the title of a file of Cavafy's poems, Ἔτη Πτερόεντα ('winged years' for Homer's ἔπεα πτερόεντα, 'winged words').[14] But we can trace the modes of misquotation back into modern Greek poetry. K. Th. Dimarás comments on a poem of 1817 by George Sakellários (1765–1838):

> The 'Night the First' is adorned with a [misspelt] motto from *Odyssey* Book 11 [182–3]:
>
> For me the miserable
> nights and days are constantly waning as I shed tears.
>
> We see here the typical way in which the pre-Romantic poet fitted the Homeric epics to his own world. And, in the first place, the Homeric text, by the alteration Sakellarios makes in it, becomes much more subjective; it takes on a purely Romantic feeling. The ancient passage is taken from the part where Odysseus is hearing from his mother the description of Penelope's life in Ithaca. It is to Penelope, consequently, and not to the narrator, that the verses apply: their correct form is
>
> For her the miserable
> nights and days are constantly waning as she sheds tears.
>
> So Homer becomes a sort of precursor of weepy Romantic and pre-Romantic self-description, a precursor of Young.[15]

We find the same move in the title of Vasiliadis' collection, Ἔπεα Πτερόεντα (1872): here the Homeric quotation is given a particular twist by the motto placed beneath it, '"Words, words!"

[13] Mimnermus, poem 2; incidentally quoted by Yannis Dallas, Καβάφης καὶ ἱστορία (Athens 1974), p. 83.

[14] G. P. Savidis, Οἱ Καβαφικὲς ἐκδόσεις (1891–1932) (Athens 1966), p. 137.

[15] Dimaras, Ἑλληνικός ρωμαντισμός, pp. 52–3.

(Shakespeare)'.[16] This second quotation, also out of context, makes the Homeric epithet take on the meaning 'winged' in the sense of fleeting and pointless. This sort of Romantic misquotation is a venerable tradition made popular (in Greece, among other places) by Edward Young's *Night Thoughts*: a healthy survivor is the Virgilian 'sunt lacrimae rerum et mentem mortalia tangunt'.[17] It is to this tradition that we may compare Cavafy's early encounters with Homer; once again we may cite Sakellarios, whose 'Night the Second' is headed by the epigraph (again horribly misspelt):

> *For such is the mind of earthly men*
> *for the day that the father of gods and men brings on.*
>
> HOMER *Odyssey* Book 18 [136–7]

Later he continues his reflections as follows:

> Various ideas come into my mind,
> sundry suspicions tyrannize me.
> Therefore I seek an outlet for emotion in books;
> at once I find Homer before me.
> I open Book 18 of the *Odyssey*, as luck would have it,
> and read with great attention.
> And in that great and foremost of poets
> I have found no little consolation for my pain.
> Especially when I have found him too saying
> that the life of men is unstable, susceptible of alteration,
> and they change their mood and character continually
> as the wheel of fortune carries them round.
> While I summon to mind the poet's verses
> I recollect my many sufferings.[18]

Although Cavafy may never have read Sakellarios, there are here certain affinities in metre and mood; and the above passage may help us to think again about the nature of Homeric allusion in Cavafy.

A famous example of Cavafian misquotation, this time in his

[16] Παπαρρηγόπουλος–Βασιλειάδης (Βασική Βιβλιοθήκη), p. 204; the words from *Troilus* 5.3.108 or *Hamlet* 2.2.195.

[17] On Young in Greece see Dimaras, Ἱστορία, p. 559.

[18] Yeóryios Sakellários, Ποιημάτια (Vienna 1817), pp. 45, 47.

collected poems, is 'Che Fece ... Il Gran Rifiuto'. The poet's editor writes:

> the dots show that Cavafy omitted these words ['per viltà'] justifiably (and on this point I disagree with the continuation of Seferis' note), because he is not interpreting Dante but simply borrowing an expression for the title of a totally unrelated poem.

But borrowing from where? Seferis was probably right in suggesting an English provenance for the deliberate misquotation.[19] But this is not the reason for his austerity: he is rather in agreement with Eliot's famous statement that 'bad poets deface what they take' – a comment that fits like a glove the untalented early Cavafy.[20]

The question that arises is whether we can't extend our observations about blatant misquotation to other cases in which a passage of Homer is out of context. The section that follows develops the defence of 'Che Fece' into an admission that Cavafy's 'Homeric' poems are in an important sense unrelated to Homer: we may take up Seferis' point that 'Che Fece' is the only poem in which Cavafy quotes from an author in a foreign language. Now the *prima facie* sign of identity of language will be *verbatim* quotation – but of quotation from the Homeric poems we find all too little in Cavafy.[21] Still, there is no reason why we should be disconcerted by Cavafy's small Greek and less Latin.

[19] Cavafy's poem in Ποιήματα vol. 1, p. 104; Savidis' comment in Μικρὰ Καβαφικά vol. 1 (Athens 1985), pp. 60–1; the discussion by Seferis in Δοκιμές vol. 1, pp. 388–92; a precursor, or at least a parallel, is John Ruskin, *Sesame and Lilies* (London 1884), §73.

[20] Eliot, *Sacred Wood*, p. 125.

[21] Cavafy's «Πριάμου νυκτοπορία» (Ἀνέκδοτα ποιήματα, pp. 51–5), in which some words from Homer are repeated *verbatim*, is essentially an unfinished poem which is cannibalized by 'The Horses of Achilles' and 'Trojans'.

Chapter Eight
Ancient days

I

At one stage Cavafy grouped several poems together, for his own reference, under the heading 'Ancient Days'; one of the best known is 'The Horses of Achilles' (1897):

> When they saw Patroclus slain,
> who was so brave, and strong, and young,
> the horses of Achilles began to weep;
> their immortal nature was exasperated
> at the work of death which it beheld.
> They tossed their heads and shook their long manes,
> struck the ground with their feet, and mourned
> Patroclus, whom they felt lifeless – wiped out –
> a worthless piece of flesh now – his spirit gone –
> defenceless – without breath –
> sent back from life to the great Nothing.
>
> Zeus saw the immortal horses'
> tears and took pity. 'At Peleus' wedding',
> he said, 'I should not have acted so thoughtlessly;
> better not to have given you away, my unhappy
> horses! What were you about down there
> among the wretched human race that is the toy of fate?
> You who are not watched over by death, or by old age,
> are being tyrannized by temporary misfortunes. Men have tangled
> you in their sufferings.' – But the two noble beasts
> continued to shed their tears
> for the permanent misfortune of death.[1]

D. N. Maronitis has written acutely about this poem on the assumption that it alludes directly to Homer; but we can challenge the assumption by comparing the poem with the relevant Homeric

[1] 'Ancient Days' is Cavafy's title for a category of his poems (Savidis, Οἱ Καβαφικὲς ἐκδόσεις, p. 137), one of which is «Τὰ ἄλογα τοῦ Ἀχιλλέως», Ποιήματα vol. 1, p. 113. It will be clear that my discussion is indebted to the study by Maronitis, «Τὰ Καβαφικὰ '῎Αλογα'».

passage (*Iliad* 17.424–58) – significant verbal echoes are not to be found – and with Pope's translation, which Cavafy owned. Achilles' friend Patroclus has been killed by Hector while wearing Achilles' armour and using his horses; battle begins over the corpse.

Meantime, at distance from the Scene of Blood,
The pensive Steeds of great *Achilles* stood;
Their god-like Master slain before their Eyes,
They wept, and shar'd in human Miseries.
In vain *Automedon* now shakes the Rein,
Now plies the Lash, and sooths and threats in vain;
Nor to the Fight, nor *Hellespont*, they go;
Restive they stood, and obstinate in Woe:
Still as a Tomb-stone, never to be mov'd,
On some good Man, or Woman unreprov'd
Lays its eternal Weight; or fix'd as stands
A marble courser by the Sculptor's Hands,
Plac'd on the Hero's Grave. Along their Face,
The big round Drops cours'd down with silent pace,
Conglobing on the Dust. Their Manes, that late
Circled their arching Necks, and wav'd in State,
Trail'd on the Dust beneath the Yoke were spread,
And prone to Earth was hung their languid Head:
Nor *Jove* disdain'd to cast a pitying Look,
While thus relenting to the Steeds he spoke.
Unhappy Coursers of immortal Strain!
Exempt from Age, and deathless now in vain;
Did we your race on mortal Man bestow,
Only alas! to share in mortal Woe?
For ah! what is there, of inferior Birth,
That breathes or creeps upon the Dust of Earth;
What wretched Creature of what wretched kind,
Than Man more weak, calamitous, and blind?
A miserable Race! But cease to mourn.
For not by you shall *Priam*'s Son be born
High on the splendid Car: One glorious Prize
He rashly boasts; the rest our Will denies.

Ourself will Swiftness to your Nerves impart,
Ourself with rising Spirits swell your Heart.
Automedon your rapid Flight shall bear
Safe to the Navy through the Storm of War.
For yet 'tis giv'n to *Troy* to ravage o'er
The Field, and spread her Slaughters to the Shore;
The Sun shall see her conquer, till his Fall
With sacred Darkness shades the Face of all.
He said; and breathing in th' immortal Horse
Excessive Spirit, urged 'em to the Course;
From their high Manes they shake the Dust, and bear
The kindling Chariot thro' the parted War.[2]

This long passage of Pope leaves traces in Cavafy's poem, giving it much of its colouring – a hue not in Homer's *Iliad*. The key words of Pope that are not in Homer but which dominate Cavafy's poem are these: 'and shar'd in human Miseries'; the 'Work of Death' so prominent in Cavafy appears in Pope's rendering of the last line of Book 17; and the concatenation of phrases about the dead Patroclus is also culled from Pope (Book 16, lines 552, 1017, 1000, 1032): 'the breathless body'; 'with faint expiring Breath'; 'So many Lives effused, expires his own'; 'the beauteous Body left a Load of Clay'. So much for the poem's tone – but what about its shape? To what does Cavafy owe its most prominent feature, the cutting short of Zeus' speech?

It was suggested earlier that the taking of a passage out of context might amount to a form of misquotation: the shading from the former into the latter can, once again, be illustrated from Sakellarios. He places the following (again misspelt) epigraph at the head of a poem lamenting his dead wife (*Odyssey* 4.195–8):

I do not begrudge
weeping over a mortal who dies and follows his fate.
For this is the prerogative of wretched mortals,
to tear their hair and shed tears from their cheeks.[3]

[2] Pope, *The Iliad of Homer* Book 17, lines 484–527.
[3] Sakellarios, Ποιημάτια, p. 7.

This passage, excised from its context, looks like an endorsement of unremitting grief: in context, it is answered by the common sense of Menelaus (*Odyssey* 4.212–13):

> But let us have an end to the weeping which came about earlier, and let us take thought of the feast.

The refusal to allow what Homer resolves find a resolution in a new poem is shared by Cavafy, whose unfinished poem 'The Night Journey of Priam' (1893) freezes the episode in which Priam goes to ransom his son's body at its most doubtful moment – and this clearly anticipates the technique of 'The Horses'. But it is the English literary background that will take us further in the understanding of that poem: the Horses of Achilles figure prominently in the writings of Victorian men of letters known to Cavafy. Arnold in his lecture on translating Homer makes the episode one of the touchstones by which the greatness of the *Iliad* is to be judged; Pater comments on the scene as exemplary; most significantly, Ruskin declares:

> There is, perhaps, in all the *Iliad* nothing more deep in significance – there is nothing in all literature more perfect in human tenderness and honour for the mystery of inferior life – than the verses that describe the sorrow of the divine horses on the death of Patroclus, and the comfort given them by the greatest of the gods.[4]

The last phrase here enables us to put our finger on the character of Cavafy's poem – but it is not a uniquely Cavafian character. Indeed, we find a close contemporary parallel in Meredith, who in 1891 published some 'Fragments of the *Iliad* in Hexameter Verse', one of which was 'The Horses of Achilles'.[5] The choice of the term 'fragments' is appropriate beyond the obvious fact that Meredith is

[4] Arnold, *Essays Literary and Critical*, pp. 239–40 (the lecture owned by Cavafy: Mihális Perídis, Ὁ βίος καὶ τὸ ἔργο τοῦ Κωνσταντίνου Καβάφη (Athens 1948), p. 68); Walter Pater, *Appreciations* (London 1924), pp. 241–61 (for Pater and Cavafy see Diana Haas, 'Early Cavafy and the European "Esoteric Movement"', *Journal of Modern Greek Studies* 2 (1984), 209–44); Ruskin, *Fors Clavigera* (London 1871–4), pp. 171–3 (on Cavafy's interest see Stratís Tsírkas, Ὁ πολιτικὸς Καβάφης (Athens 1971), pp. 222–65).

[5] George Meredith, *Poems* (London 1912), p. 426; on the technique see Maronitis, «Ὁ μυθολογικὸς Καβάφης καὶ ἡ 'Πριάμου νυκτοπορία'», Χάρτης nos. 5–6 (1983), 620–9.

translating only parts of Homer: it indicates that, by taking favoured passages out of context, the poet is really producing new works of art. And in this particular case Meredith does just what Cavafy does: he leaves out the consolatory remarks of Zeus. Cavafy's poem too is a fragment; it too is a self-contained scene, and the absence of the surrounding war context of the *Iliad* is only to be expected. The removal of Automedon also fits this pattern: Cavafy wants a direct dialogue between Zeus and the Horses without the presence of humanity. Humanity, rather – with Patroclus as the case in point – is just the subject of discussion.

The Horses are not to be consoled: this is the point of the poem. But the point is not left to speak for itself; it is explained. The Horses, like the absent Achilles himself with his divine mother Thetis and human father Peleus, are caught between divinity and humanity; and the poem's last two and a half lines, which not only conclude the narrative as altered by Cavafy but also gloss the first part of the poem as a whole, define the problem. The Horses share with man the human quality of nobility (a quality which Cavafy here and in the earlier version of 'The Funeral of Sarpedon' denies the gods); but they are unlike men, and like what we expect of the gods, in their powers of understanding. While the gods (for whom Zeus is the spokesman) can only see the temporary misfortunes of each individual death, the Horses can see the permanent misfortune of Death itself – that through which Achilles himself, the owner of the Horses, will eventually die. It is as if Cavafy has placed a very strong emphasis on Pope's epithet 'pensive' so as to make the Horses thinkers about, rather than mere feelers of, misfortune. And, as De Quincey had observed of the Homeric episode, the rationality of Achilles' Horses sits strangely with the modern Greek word for horse, ἄλογο (literally, 'irrational thing') – something to which Cavafy's title, we can now see, is evidently making reference.[6]

The poem, then, is not lacking in a rhetoric of a certain plausibility. But it is as true of 'The Horses of Achilles' as of Cavafy's earlier efforts that it is a defacing of Homer. Building a modern Greek poetic tradition which earns the right to express a debt to

[6] Thomas De Quincey, *Works* vol. 6 (Edinburgh 1890), p. 36.

Homer is a matter of facing up to the Homeric poems as they are, not as we would wish them to be; and to alter the source itself is to take a facile and unoriginal way out: it is to indulge in all the emotion that attracted Ruskin without going on to take the consolation that the poem goes on to offer. It is tempting, then, to classify 'The Horses' with the sort of poem against which T. E. Hulme inveighed: 'I object to the sloppiness which doesn't consider that a poem is a poem unless it is whining about something or other.'[7] This judgement is a harsh one, admittedly; but, while admitting it, we can nonetheless draw attention to two related elements in the poem which look forward to the second version of 'The Funeral of Sarpedon', a poem in which the Homeric questions about the relations of gods and men are handled with a greater degree of sophistication.[8] The first is something which Cavafy added to the Homeric episode; the second something which he removed.

The latent homoerotic sentiment of Cavafy's 'Horses' has been noted by Maronitis. And we can extend this observation with reference to a small detail in which Cavafy's poem differs from the *Iliad*:

> They tossed their heads and shook their long manes,
> struck the ground with their feet.

Here we have a wilder display of emotion than the drooping grief of the Horses in the *Iliad* – why? In his own search to express his feelings about the untimely death of Arthur Hallam, Tennyson too had turned (in a veiled way) to the Horses of Achilles, but had felt that grief after this sort did the emotion justice ('Tithonus' lines 39–42):

> and the wild team
> Which love thee, yearning for thy yoke, arise
> And shake the darkness from their loosened manes
> And beat the twilight into flakes of fire.[9]

[7] T. E. Hulme, *Speculations* (ed. Herbert Read, London 1960), p. 126.

[8] The same may be said of the poems «Διακοπή» and «᾿Απιστία» (Ποιήματα vol. 1, pp. 102, 109–10), which treat of divine–human relations through incidents in the margins of Homer; see on these Ricks, 'Homer and Greek Poetry', pp. 67–82.

[9] Tennyson, *Poems* vol. 2, p. 609.

But while Tennyson distanced his poem from Homer, Cavafy, unfortunately, could not distance Homer from Tennyson; and so he imported into the Homeric scene an irrelevant obsession with ageing. In the *Iliad* the Horses weep for Patroclus simply because they loved him, not because he was young (he wasn't). Only by grafting sentiments aroused by the *Iliad* into what Eliot calls 'a new whole of feeling' would Cavafy succeed, as he did in the second version of 'The Funeral of Sarpedon'.[10]

There is another direct point of comparison between 'The Horses' and 'The Funeral', and it concerns an element in the Homeric source which Cavafy excluded from his own poem, the simile of the horses as a tombstone. Maronitis' suggestion that the omission is a gesture of respect from one poet to another itself commands respect in principle; but in this case it seems unlikely to fit the facts: despite the lip-service he pays to Homer in his essay on Odysseus, we have not been able so far to see Cavafy's relations with Homer as characterized by scrupulous restraint.[11] We may rather suggest a pair of other reasons. First of all, to use the device of simile implicitly brings a context with it, while Cavafy has deliberately chosen to give us a Homeric *tableau*. Furthermore, to mention a stele (as to mention Automedon, who appears immediately before this) is to introduce a sense that life goes on – 'in the midst of death we are in life' – into a poem which wants things to be starker, which wants man to be a mere fleshly receptacle of soul. In 'The Funeral of Sarpedon', however, it is precisely that continuing life of man that receives attention; and we shall see how the funeral monument reappears in that new and appropriate context.

II

Before we leave 'The Horses of Achilles' we should look at Sikelianos' reaction to it in a poem from *Visionary* not earlier discussed, a poem with the identical title, 'The Horses of Achilles', bar the demotic forms (Τ' ἄλογα τοῦ 'Αχιλλέα). This will give us a sense

[10] Eliot, *Sacred Wood*, p. 125.

[11] Maronitis, «Τὰ Καβαφικὰ '"Αλογα'», pp. 366–7.

of how the modern Greek poets borrow from each other even when their work appears to depend directly on Homer.

> O asphodel meadow; by you
> two horses neighed
> and passed through at speed...
> Their backs shone like a wave;
> they emerged from the sea,
> cut across the deserted sand,
> with necks upright; tall, tall;
> with white foam; stallions...
> In their eyes glowed
> a flash of lightning; and they plunged
> once again into the wave, waves;
> foam in the sea's foam;
> and disappeared. And I recognized
> the steeds, of which the one took on a human,
> prophetic voice.
> The hero was holding the reins;
> he struck, urged on
> his divine youth...
>
> Holy steeds, fate
> has kept you indestructible,
> binding on your black, black foreheads,
> against impious eyes,
> a great
> white talisman![12]

This poem appears in a section of *Visionary* in which the poet is imagining himself in an asphodel meadow like that of Homer's Underworld – the place where Odysseus met an Achilles who was still a lord among the dead but who would have returned to the Upper World even as a serf (*Odyssey* 11.488–91). But it is clear here that Sikelianos is celebrating rather his own powers of imagination in the recreation of the Homeric Underworld than the sense of loss which is actually so prominent in the Homeric picture of it. The very syntax of his poem on the Horses declares that they are at one

[12] Sikelianos, Λυρικὸς βίος vol. 1, pp. 153–4.

with Nature; and here a point so obvious that we may miss it should be made. The very fact that the Horses are still perceived as being with Achilles in the Underworld indicates that for Sikelianos – in contrast to the Homeric episode, let alone to Cavafy's development of it – the divine Horses and their mortal owner belong to the same order. This is in sharp and conscious opposition to Cavafy's poem, where it is precisely the Horses' failure to fit the natural order as understood by Zeus that is valued by the poet and taken to be the sign of their understanding of the human condition. Cavafy's 'Horses' had been singled out for praise in an early review of Cavafy in 1903; we know too that Sikelianos admired the poem; and there is no reason to doubt that the younger poet's 'Horses' represents a respectful response to Cavafy's use of the same mythical beasts.[13]

Sikelianos' Horses appear at speed with great suddenness and pass by with a flash: the rapidity of these short rhyming lines of description contrasts with the lingering lines of Cavafy's expatiation on a single, eternalized moment from the *Iliad* – the difference, as it were, between a still photograph and a motion picture. A further difference is in the use of the word ἄτια: steeds, unlike horses, are specifically heroic and do not play on the λόγος etymology; and Sikelianos is commending not reason but heroism. Again, the horse's human voice here stresses not its affinity with humanity but the opposite: the adjective μάντισσα qualifies the voice as supernaturally prophetic, deriving as it does from Homer's verb μαντεύεαι (*Iliad* 19.420) in the passage where the horse Xanthus prophesies Achilles' death to him. This second appearance of the Horses in the *Iliad* plays no part in Cavafy's poem, for obvious reasons; a further attraction for Sikelianos, as he seeks to define his poem against Cavafy's, is that the speaking horse is familiar from folk songs of a heroic cast – a tradition that has little, if anything, to do with Cavafy's Homerica. Finally, reinforcing the differences between these two modern revivals of the Horses, we have the revival of Achilles himself, conspicuous by his absence from Cavafy's poem. Sikelianos chooses to emphasize the hero's youth not as

[13] The early review: Grigóris Ksenópulos, «Ένας ποιητής» (1903), repr. in Άπαντα (Athens 1972) vol. 11, pp. 51–60; Sikelianos on the poem in Πεζὸς λόγος vol. 4, p. 88.

vulnerable but as godlike; and the hero is not only seen but seen in action as the poem ends with an echo of the last line of Book 19 of the *Iliad*, at the point at which Achilles begins his avenging drive against the Trojans in earnest:

> He spoke, and with a yell in the front rank drove his uncloven-footed horses on.

Sikelianos puts the heroism back into a subject from which Cavafy had removed it; and it is characteristic that the poem ends as it begins with the Horses' physical attributes. For Cavafy these are significant only insofar as they are revealing of human emotions: for Sikelianos, by contrast, the white mark on the Horses' heads is at once a celebration of their physical existence and, in terms of folk belief, the plain sign that they are not 'the toy of Fate'.

III

A passage of the *Iliad* comparable to that from which 'The Horses of Achilles' was taken became in the hands of Cavafy a much more complex poem, 'The Funeral of Sarpedon' (1908):

> Zeus is greatly pained. Sarpedon
> has been slain by Patroclus; and now
> Menoetius' son and the Achaeans rush on
> to snatch the body and degrade it.
>
> But Zeus is not at all disposed to allow this.
> His beloved child – whom he let
> be lost; such was Law –
> he will at least honour in death.
> And lo, he sends Phoebus down to the field
> with orders to look after the body.
>
> Phoebus lifts the hero's corpse,
> with piety and grief, and takes it to the river.
> He washes it of the dust and the blood;
> he closes the terrible wounds, not allowing
> any trace to be visible; he pours
> scents of ambrosia over him; and clothes him

with shining Olympian garments.
He whitens his skin; and with a pearl
comb combs the dark black hair.
He arranges and lays out the beautiful limbs.

Now he looks like a young king charioteer –
at twenty-five years of age, at twenty-six –
resting after he has won
with his golden chariot and swiftest horses
the prize in a famous contest.

So when Phoebus had fulfilled
his orders, he called the two brothers,
Sleep and Death, commanding them
to take the body to Lycia, the rich land.

And over there, to the rich land Lycia,
these two brothers escorted him,
Sleep and Death, and when they eventually reached
the door of the royal house
they handed over the glorious body,
and went back to their other concerns and tasks.

And when they had received the corpse there, at home,
with processions, and honours, and lamentations,
and abundant libations from sacred bowls,
and with everything fitting, the mournful burial began;
and later experienced craftsmen from the city
and reputed workers in stone
came and made the tomb and monument.[14]

In the form in which it first appeared in 1898, 'The Funeral of Sarpedon' was, like 'The Horses', too intimately connected to Pope's *Iliad*; but, having learned much in the following decade, Cavafy returned to the poem and produced a new version of it which deserves to be called a new poem. Justification for dwelling on it in some detail is provided in part by the need for a corrective to the influential view of Seferis, who underestimated the poem. It can be argued that 'The Funeral''s very individuality made it less

[14] Cavafy, «Ἡ κηδεία τοῦ Σαρπηδόνος», Ποιήματα vol. 1, pp. 111–12.

easily assimilable to the later poet's picture of Cavafy; and its literary background, which was unfamiliar to Seferis, makes it rather easier to understand. Above all, Seferis was mistaken in thinking that comparison of the 1898 and 1908 versions was a waste of time: the very anomalousness of the poem's status in Cavafy's *œuvre* – we are at the borders of revision and rewriting – is an indication that it is here, above all, that Cavafy's struggle with the problem of Homeric allusion is conducted.[15]

As it happens, we know what Cavafy's original inspiration for the poem was: a painting which portrayed Sleep and Death conveying Sarpedon from the field. Cavafy was attracted by this frankly homoerotic scene, and he attempted to develop it into a poem by mining Pope's account of the episode.[16] As with 'The Horses' we can set Cavafy's 1898 text next to Pope's and the attentive reader will find a number of borrowings:

> Zeus' heart is full of pain.
> Patroclus has slain Sarpedon.
>
> The God has respected the will of Fate.
> But the father mourns his misfortune.
>
> Menoetius' unconquerable son,
> the Achaeans roaring like lions,
> are seeking to snatch the dead man and throw him
> to crows and dogs as food.
>
> But Zeus is not disposed to allow this humiliation.
> His dear and honoured son's
> body he will not allow them to insult.
>
> Lo, from his chariot Phoebus descends
> to earth, at Zeus' orders.
> The divine hands rescue Sarpedon's
> corpse, and take him to
> the river and wash him piously.

15 Seferis, Δοκιμές vol. 1, p. 402; on the text of the poem see Savidis, «'Επτὰ στάδια ἑνὸς ποιήματος τοῦ Καβάφη ('Ἡ κηδεία τοῦ Σαρπηδόνος') (1892–1924)», in *Lirica Greca da Archiloco a Elitis. Studi in onore di Filippo Maria Pontani* (Padua 1984), pp. 341–57.

16 It is interesting that Pope, too, felt a special affinity for the Sarpedon episode, translating it before the rest of the *Iliad*: see the *Poems* (ed. John Butt, London 1961), pp. 60–9, with the discussion by Reuben A. Brower, *Alexander Pope: the Poetry of Allusion* (Oxford 1959), pp. 85–141.

The dust and clotted blood are cleansed away,
and the just, brave hero's
physiognomy appears to view.
Phoebus liberally pours the scents
of ambrosia over the corpse
and covers it with Olympian,
immortal garments. He closes
the chest's gaping wound. He gives
a peaceful and graceful arrangement to his limbs.
The skin takes on a brightness. A shining comb
combs his locks, abundant locks
and black, not yet dishonoured
by a single white hair.
He appears as a young athlete
resting – as a young lover
dreaming of joy and cupids
with azure wings and heavenly
bows – as a young and happy spouse,
lucky among all his peers,
who has won a lovely bride without bride-price.

Having carried out his orders, the God
calls on the brothers Sleep and Death,
and orders that Sarpedon
be conveyed to broad Lycia.

As if in a tender paternal embrace,
Sleep and Death took him
with grief and with love and with care
lest the dead face's serious calm,
be disturbed; lest the grandeur
of the virile body be impaired.

The Lycians made deep bows
to the Gods of fearful insensibility,
and received their fine lord
dead in spirit but glorious in form,
in his prime, and fragrant, and peaceful.

They set up to him a marble monument,
and on its base in relief
experienced craftsmen carved the hero's
victories and his many campaigns.[17]

The whole episode is clearly based on that narrated in Book 16 of the *Iliad*: Zeus is troubled at the impending death of his son Sarpedon and thinks aloud about saving him; Hera resists this challenge to the established order, but allows that the body at least be rescued from dishonour; later Apollo brings this about. The relevant passages of Pope read as follows:

Jove view'd the Combate, whose Event foreseen,
He thus bespoke his Sister and his Queen.
The Hour draws on; the Destinies ordain,
My godlike Son shall press the Phrygian Plain:
Already on the Verge of Death he stands,
His Life is ow'd to fierce *Patroclus*' Hands.
What Passions in a Parent's Breast debate!
Say, shall I snatch him from impending Fate,
And send him safe to *Lycia*, distant far
From all the Dangers and the Toils of War;
Or to his Doom my bravest Offspring yield,
And fatten, with celestial Blood, the Field?
  Then thus the Goddess with the radiant Eyes:
What words are these, O Sov'reign of the Skies?
Short is the Date prescribed to mortal Man;
Shall *Jove*, for one, extend the narrow Span,
Whose Bounds were fixed before his Race began?
How many Sons of Gods, foredoom'd to Death,
Before proud *Ilion*, must resign their Breath!
Were thine exempt, Debate would rise above,
And murm'ring Pow'rs condemn their partial *Jove*.
Give the bold chief a glorious Fate in fight;
And when th'ascending Soul has wing'd her flight,
Let *Sleep* and *Death* convey, by thy Command,
The breathless Body to his native Land.

[17] Cavafy, Ἀποκηρυγμένα, pp. 56–8.

His Friends and People, to his future Praise,
A marble Tomb and Pyramid shall raise,
And lasting Honours to his Ashes give;
His Fame ('tis all the Dead can have!) shall live.
She said; the Cloud-compeller overcome,
Assents to Fate, and ratifies the Doom.
Then, touch'd with Grief, the weeping Heav'ns distill'd
A show'r of Blood o'er all the fatal Field.
The God, his Eyes averting from the Plain,
Laments his Son, predestin'd to be slain,
Far from the Lycian Shores, his happy native Reign.

. . .

Then thus to *Phoebus*, in the Realms above,
Spoke from his Throne the Cloud-compelling *Jove*.
Descend, my *Phoebus*! on the *Phrygian* Plain,
And from the Fight convey *Sarpedon* slain;
Then bathe his Body in the crystal Flood,
With Dust dishonour'd, and deform'd with Blood:
O'er all his Limbs Ambrosial Odours shed,
And with celestial Robes adorn the Dead.
These Rites discharg'd, his sacred Corpse bequeath
To the soft Arms of silent *Sleep* and *Death*;
They to his Friends the mournful Charge shall bear,
His Friends a Tomb and Pyramid shall rear;
What Honours Mortals after Death receive,
Those unavailing Honours we may give!
Apollo bows, and from Mount *Ida*'s Height
Swift to the Field precipitates his Flight;
Thence from the War the breathless Hero bore,
Veil'd in a Cloud, to silver *Simois*' Shore:
There bath'd his honourable Wounds, and drest
His manly Members in th'immortal Vest;
And with Perfumes of sweet Ambrosial Dews,
Restores his Freshness, and his Form renews.
There *Sleep* and *Death*, two twins of winged Race,
Of matched Swiftness, but of silent Pace,
Receiv'd *Sarpedon*, at the God's Command,

And in a Moment reached the *Lycian* land.
The Corpse among his weeping Friends they laid,
Where endless Honours wait the sacred Shade.[18]

There is not space here to dwell on all the ways in which Cavafy's later version is superior: our subject, in any case, is not the poet's idiosyncratic development but – more impersonally – the ways in which the short poem in modern Greek can allude to Homer and yet escape his shadow.[19] The most marked difference, to be seen from a glance at the two versions, is one of scale: the 1908 version has only 42 lines to the earlier version's 55. But there is a greater statistical disparity which indicates a qualitative difference also: the 1908 version has only 20 adjectives to the 1898 version's 39. Even the linguistic side of revision, then, has a particular slant, the removal or alteration of Popean epithets – some of which (like 'marble' at the poem's end) are not in Homer at all. This revision is certainly in accordance with the general precepts of Cavafy's mature art; but it is specifically an attempt to escape the influence of Homer, strangely refracted as it has been by Cavafy's translation of Pope's epithets into a slightly archaizing Greek.[20] A contemporary remark by Pound is illuminating:

> Don't allow 'influence' to mean merely that you mop up the particular decorative vocabulary of some one or two poets whom you happen to admire. A Turkish war correspondent was recently caught red-handed babbling in his despatches of 'dove-grey' hills, or else it was 'pearl-pink', I can not remember.[21]

It is significant, perhaps – and it does something to bear out Seferis' hunch that Cavafy's Homeric poems have something to do with the publication of Pallis' fine demotic *Iliad* (first instalment 1892) – that one way in which the 1908 'Funeral' moves away from a trite,

[18] Pope, *Iliad* Book 16, lines 528–63, 809–36; in addition to these two passages note the following phrases from Pope's translation of Book 16 which are in Cavafy's poem but not in the Homeric original: 'the wide Wound' (623), 'clotted blood' (637), 'Menaetius' Son' (755).

[19] Savidis, «Ἑπτὰ στάδια» reveals that the poem continued to grow after 1908, but the traditional date for the later version, 1908, is the one that will be referred to here.

[20] See Cavafy's so-called 'Ars Poetica', ed. A. Decavalles, *The Charioteer* 10 (1968), 69–80.

[21] Pound, *Literary Essays* (ed. T. S. Eliot, London 1985), p. 5.

'poetic' idiom and eschews the manner Homeric themes seem to impose, is in borrowing from Pallis' translation.[22]

A more general difference between the versions – a 'philosophical' difference, to use Cavafy's working definition in what has come to be known as his *Ars Poetica* – confronts us at the very beginning with the now less violent emotions of Zeus. This is a sign that Cavafy has learned not to accept or reject Homer's terms outright but rather – to adapt Forster's famous remark about the poet – to stand at a slight angle to them; and we shall find confirmation of this in various aspects of his new poem. That the case with which the poem deals is a classic one is shown by Plato's attention to it in the *Republic* (388b):

> And all the more shall we ask [of the poets] not to have the gods mourning... and if the gods at all, then certainly not to dare to imitate in such an unseemly fashion the greatest of the gods [as here:]...
>
> Woe is me, for it is the fate of Sarpedon, dearest to me of all men to be vanquished by Patroclus, son of Menoetius.

It is in fact to be doubted whether 'The Funeral' is directly related to this passage, but it hardly matters. We shall note at a later point a striking instance of Cavafy's finding his own devious way back to the old Homeric problems.

IV

Could 'The Horses' ever have been redeemed as a poem? Possibly not. But while 'The Funeral', too, began life as an affecting Homeric *tableau*, similarly expanded by recourse to Pope, its very confusion – as opposed to 'The Horses'' clarity – meant that it was possible to improve it. What had drawn Cavafy in 1892 was the thought of a young man's being given a divine funeral (κηδεία) and the caring attention (the cognate κήδομαι) of Apollo: by 1908 the poet was ready to do justice to the particular status of Sarpedon as bridging the divine and human worlds.

[22] Pallis, Ἰλιάδα (1904), 16.447, 451, 673–4, 678–9; the book was owned by Cavafy: see Peridis, Βίος καὶ ἔργο, p. 67.

The poet has now clarified considerably his account of the relations between gods and men. In the first place, explicit criticisms of the gods disappear: Cavafy does not try to iron out the difficulties caused the gods by their sons of mixed parentage – this, through Achilles, is the narrative backbone of the *Iliad* – but makes clear the two levels, divine and human, at which Sarpedon is honoured. So now there is no need either to accuse the gods of being lacking in feeling or to make Zeus appear more grieved than he really is: Zeus' activity ('mourns') is turned into an uncomfortable but transitory state ('is greatly pained'). Furthermore, the abrupt contrast between gods and men disappears, as does the word 'god' altogether: this makes it the clearer that Zeus is pressing on with his duty to honour Sarpedon with first Apollo, then Sleep and Death, as his agents; he is not guilty of parental neglect. Cavafy, in the later version, sees Zeus' mixed feelings but wishes to explain them by a coherent theology.

The simpler language at the beginning of Cavafy's 1908 version, then, is the sign of more than changed linguistic views. The phrase

> ποὺ τὸ ἄφισε
> καὶ χάθηκεν· ὁ Νόμος ἦταν ἔτσι

describes Zeus' abandonment of Sarpedon in simple but not callous terms. Cavafy has made the precedence of super-divine Law so obvious to Zeus that it need be mentioned but parenthetically; he need not therefore condemn the gods for what takes place or switch the poem back and forth between divine and human stages. Much is of course left for a subject: the poet's initial fascination with the divine and human funerals of Sarpedon, the former despite his mortality and the latter to give him immortality in human terms, continues to be his preoccupation in the later version of the poem.

There, as has been pointed out, the gods do not appear as a class; but neither does Sarpedon appear by name except in the initial statement of his death: instead of 'Sarpedon's corpse' we now have 'the hero's corpse'. This anonymity makes more universal the poem's treatment of mortality; but Zeus' care, through the other gods, for his son is not suppressed but made rather more perspicuous than it was in the feeble *variatio* of the 1898 version. Apollo is now the subject of all the verbs for the divine funeral, emphasizing the unusual nature of the ceremony: it is one which we expect to be performed by a woman (characteristically a mother). Among the fussy and value-laden details which Cavafy suppresses from this later version the most obtrusive is that of the hair ἣν ἔτι δὲν ἠτίμασε | λευκή τις θρίξ. While the other details are trite and vague, this is a more serious flaw in the poem, for it recalls and trivializes another passage of Homer (Pope, *Iliad* 22.207–9) which describes the body of Hector:

> The Face divine and long-descending Hair
> Purple the Ground, and streak the sable Sand;
> Deformed, dishonoured, in his native Land.

With this passage at the back of our minds, Cavafy's lines are the intrusion of an alien and unattractive obsession. But in the 1908 version the poet not only avoids this bathos but replaces it with vivid touches which are characteristic of much of his work. For example, he develops Pope's references to *form* in order to make Sarpedon's an ideal body. Instead of the three heterogeneous commonplaces about a typical youth Cavafy now supplies us with a specific age – as so often in his erotic poems – and a specific scene which is both more tellingly Homeric and less obtrusively so than the mention of 'bride-price'. For we may discern the origins of the new picture in these lines describing the pursuit of Hector by Achilles (Pope, *Iliad* 22.211–14):

> As when some Hero's Fun'rals are decreed
> In grateful Honour of the mighty Dead;
> Where high Rewards the Vig'rous Youth inflame,
> (Some golden Tripod or some lovely Dame).

We come now to the second half of 'The Funeral', in which Sleep and Death take over from Apollo and bear Sarpedon home. Their sole attribute in Homer is their speed, and Cavafy's initial attribution of emotions to them (in this he follows Pope) is intended to do anything but soften the blow of mortality. In the 1908 version, by contrast, Cavafy acknowledges the gap between gods and men by making it clear that Sarpedon was swiftly deposited in Lycia by divine agents with other business in hand; and his throwaway phrase of explanation – like the earlier line about Law – is a verse which is not so much callous as breezily consoling in tone:

καὶ γύρισαν στὲς ἄλλες τους φροντίδες καὶ δουλειές.

It is significant, moreover, that in the later version Sarpedon is left *at the door* of the royal house; significant, too, that the suppression of a Sleep and Death with human emotions brings with it the suppression of the Lycians themselves: an unidentified third-person plural takes up the accusative pronoun that we have followed through several stanzas. The austerity of the treatment here is indicative not just of a wish to avoid sentimentality but of a concentration on a central point: 'human immortality'. For Cavafy's poem in its new and coherent rewriting is an exploration of Juno's concluding words in Pope:

His Fame ('tis all the Dead can have!) shall live.

Hence the differences between the two versions in their treatment of the memorial. In the 1898 version the restriction to the monument alone at once admitted irrelevant detail and omitted important components of a human funeral which would balance the divine funeral already witnessed. In the 1908 version, by contrast, the monument, not described, is only the last and most lasting element of the human funeral: the tomb and stele which were removed from 'The Horses' have now returned, with a prosaic restraint from which Seferis could not withhold his admiration, as a celebration of the artist's vocation.[23]

V

Only a few aspects of the two versions of 'The Funeral' have been examined, and the above remarks have been restricted to showing how Cavafy comes to adjust his use of Homer. In the earlier version, as in 'The Horses', Cavafy simply takes a Homeric scene and grafts

[23] Seferis, Δοκιμές vol. 1, p. 402; for the sculptor as artist see most famously Cavafy's poem «Τυανεὺς γλύπτης», Ποιήματα vol. 1, pp. 41–2.

onto it a moral of his own: in the later, he has shown himself capable of assimilating Homeric material to a form that does justice to the problem of mortality. The verse, for example, is no longer strict blank verse, so that on the one hand we avoid verse clichés like the jingling balance of

> νεκρὸν τὸ πνεῦμα, ἀλλὰ τὴν μορφὴν λαμπρόν
>
> (*'dead in spirit but glorious in form'*)

and on the other meet with the deceptively casual

> καὶ γύρισαν στὲς ἄλλες τους φροντίδες καὶ δουλειές.

Once again, a declaration by Pound, writing in 1911–12, gives us an insight into Cavafy's technique:

> I should like to break up ... lines composed of two very nearly equal sections, each containing a noun and each noun decorously attended by a carefully selected epithet gleaned apparently from Shakespeare, Pope or Horace. For it is not until poetry lives again 'close to the thing' that it will be a vital part of contemporary life.[24]

These formal alterations, as we have seen, are the transformation of a hackneyed anthropocentrism, or even anthropolatry, into an acceptance of mortality that allows at the same time a kind of human immortality. It is interesting to note that, in striving to reach an understanding of – and, as a poet, with – the Sarpedon episode, Cavafy grapples with – and poetically resolves – an ancient problem. For the Scholiast had asked, 'Was not Zenodotus perhaps right to athetize these lines [*Iliad* 16.466–83]? For it is unnatural to find these tasks being performed by one who is not the one bereaved [that is, by Apollo].'[25] In 'The Funeral of Sarpedon' the divine and human ceremonies are firmly complementary.

Let us conclude by tying up a few threads. We may claim to have rebutted Seferis' remark that comparing the two versions of 'The

[24] Pound, *Selected Prose 1909–65* (ed. William Cookson, London 1973), p. 41.

[25] Erbse, *Scholia in Iliadem* on 16.466–83.

Funeral' was a waste of time. But Seferis also brought the poem into one of his most wide-ranging statements about Cavafy's work:

> [in] what I call the pseudo-historical poems ... the reference to the historian or ancient writer serves only to provide a 'subject' for the poem. Of this kind are, for example, the Homeric themes ... all you need in mind is the material coordination of the myth; you do not need, say, to know Homer well in order to appreciate – if it's worth appreciating – 'The Funeral'; indeed the vivid recollection of the *Iliad* may be detrimental.[26]

What Seferis says is, I think, true of 'The Horses', which is easily erased from the memory by the recollection of Homer; but in 'The Funeral' Seferis picked a bad example: Cavafy has genuinely succeeded in making this poem immune to the Homeric influence. Maronitis sums up the achievement as follows:

> The second and definitive version of 'The Funeral' differs in many respects from the first, but particularly in that it sets in relief the beauty of the young Sarpedon, of the corpse ... The idol of the Cavafian young body has now found its erotic discourse in the mythological climate and the mythological context.[27]

We may equally turn this around to say that Cavafy's Sarpedon has found his way out of the battlefield into the city, Cavafy's natural habitat; and out of Homer into the timeless world, on which Cavafy draws so much, of Greek epigram. The dual funeral of Sarpedon that initially interested Cavafy has been recreated in such a way as to achieve independence from the Homeric frame of reference: 'The good poet', as Eliot put it, 'welds his theft into a whole of feeling which is unique, utterly different from that from which it was torn.'[28]

It was wise of Cavafy to stick with Sarpedon rather than to attempt a similar poem with Achilles as its subject. Sarpedon is not so central to the *Iliad*; he is a Lycian, peripheral, like Cavafy's favoured subjects, to Greece proper; he is not a focus of national

[26] Seferis, Δοκιμές vol. 1, p. 435.

[27] Maronitis, «Κ. Π. Καβάφης», pp. 71–2.

[28] Eliot, *Sacred Wood*, p. 125.

aspirations. Peripheral to poetry – contrast the 1898 version's obtrusive 'victories' and Sikelianos' 'Secret Iliad' – Sarpedon looks forward to the more celebrated poem 'Caesarion'. Cavafy's achievement is to have taken a case from the *Iliad* susceptible to his distinctive historian's treatment and thereby to have found for his new poem a place outside the shadow of Homer. What Eliot wrote of a very different contemporary work, Pound's *Homage to Sextus Propertius*, may serve as the most delicate appraisal of 'The Funeral of Sarpedon':

> It is impossible, of course, to employ the words 'translation', 'original' or 'derivative' in dealing with a poem like this. Certainly there is no other poet living who could justify such a method; but we believe that Mr Pound has succeeded.[29]

[29] Eliot, 'The Method of Mr Pound', *The Athenaeum* Oct. 24 1919, 1065–6.

Chapter Nine
Homer into history

I

Cataloguing Cavafy's poems on Homeric themes, Seferis placed 'Ithaca' last and declared, 'Thereafter Homer disappears from his *œuvre.*' But this is not strictly true; and by looking at the matter briefly we shall be able to preserve the truth in Seferis' insight that Cavafy abandoned Homer while significantly modifying it. Cavafy's last poem which we can relate to Homer is 'Caesarion':[1]

> Partly to verify a date,
> partly to pass the time,
> last night I took down a collection
> of Ptolemaic inscriptions for my reading.
> The abundant encomia and the flattering words
> are much the same for all of them. All are illustrious,
> distinguished, mighty, beneficent;
> each of their enterprises most wise.
> As for the women of the line, they too,
> all the Berenices and Cleopatras, admirable.
>
> On managing to verify the date,
> I should have set the book aside had not a small,
> and insignificant, reference to King Caesarion
> attracted my immediate attention...
>
> And look, there you were, with your indefinable
> charm. In history only
> a few lines are to be found about you,
> and so I moulded you the more freely in my mind.
> I moulded you handsome and sensitive.
> My craft gives your face
> a dreamlike, sympathetic beauty.
> And so fully did I imagine you
> that last night, late, as my lamp
> was going out – I let it go out on purpose –

[1] Seferis' comment in Δοκιμές vol. 1, p. 398; Cavafy's «Καισαρίων» in Ποιήματα vol. 1, pp. 69–70.

I fancied that you had entered my room,
it seemed that you stood before me – just as you would have been
in conquered Alexandria,
pale and tired, ideal in your grief,
still hoping for mercy from
the base – who were a-whispering of 'too many Caesars'.

The saying about too many Caesars to which Cavafy alludes here parodies the proverbial Homeric line (*Iliad* 2.204):

οὐκ ἀγαθὸν πολυκοιρανίη· εἷς κοίρανος ἔστω

('*A multiplicity of leaders is not good; let there be one leader*')

Odysseus' words in the turbulent world of Rome after the assassination of Julius Caesar, took on a more than general force, and a pun was not resisted: οὐκ ἀγαθὸν πολυκαισαρίη. (This parody entailed the abandonment of the second half of the line – Καῖσαρ would not fit – but the first half was enough to get the point across.) So Cavafy's acknowledged source, Plutarch's *Life of Mark Antony* (§81).[2] The worldly philosopher Areius advises Octavian not to let Caesarion, Julius Caesar's putative son by Cleopatra, live, speaking of 'too many Caesars'. But Cavafy has carried out a significant modification of his source: Areius has been pluralized as 'the base'. Why?

By answering the title 'Caesarion', Πολυκαισαρίη sets a seal on the poem; it is interesting to learn that this keystone word and the pluralizing of the base, which go hand in hand, entered the poem only at a late stage in its composition.[3] Caesarion's name, a diminutive of 'Caesar', is at once a threat to his life and his attraction for the poet, whose love is inspired by an object of all-too-human dimensions. The saying that the base used to justify and bring about Caesarion's death has, paradoxically, assured him a sort of immortality – for Cavafy values just that Caesar about whom nothing is known but his name. And there is conscious paradox in making one whose name is the qualification of another name *ideal*.

So the 'small, and insignificant, reference' referred to in the poem can be read as the quotation embodied in the poem. But what has this to do with Homer? An understanding of 'Caesarion' in no way

[2] G. Lehonítis, Καβαφικὰ αὐτοσχόλια (Athens 1977), p. 33.

[3] Renata Lavagnini, 'Le varianti di *Cesarione*' in *Lirica Greca*, pp. 359–76.

depends on the knowledge that the proverb's ultimate derivation is Homer rather than, say, Theognis. The relevance of 'Caesarion' to this study is not that it constitutes Cavafy's *Nunc Dimittis* to Homer – it would be a distortion to claim that there was such a thing, or that this was it – but we are entitled to read it as an example of one way of dealing with the problem of alluding to Homer. For it can be taken as a sign of Cavafy's hard-won maturity that his poetic development has come full circle. He has returned – *via* the use of ancient mythological material – to the very words of Homer; but, instead of defacing them himself, he takes them as the years between Homer and himself have defaced them and embodies them in a new whole of feeling. The first step requires the perspicacity and detachment of the historian: Gibbon, punning on the imperial purple, cites with respect to the Emperor Julian the Homeric line,

> a purple death overcame him, and a strong fate.[4]

The second step requires the skill of a poet. The technique is, to be sure, not without its advantages for the modern Greek poet who does not move with ease through the Homeric poems themselves; but it is not just a poetic gambit but a successful response to a – peculiarly Greek – predicament which Cavafy explored in the following awkward but suggestive manuscript note:

> It is one of the talents of great stylists to make obsolete words cease from appearing obsolete through the way in which they introduce them in their writing. Obsolete words which under the pens of others would seem stilted or out of place occur most naturally under theirs. This is owing to the tact & the judgement of the writers who know when – & when only – the disused term can be introduced, when it is artistically agreeable or linguistically necessary; & of course then the obsolete word becomes obsolete only in name. It is recalled into existence by the natural requirements of a powerful or subtle style. It is not a corpse disinterred (as with less skillful writers) but a beautiful body awaked from a long and refreshing sleep.[5]

[4] Edward Gibbon, *The Decline and Fall of the Roman Empire* (London 1954), vol. 2, p. 188; for Cavafy's interest see Diana Haas, 'Cavafy's Reading Notes on Gibbon's *Decline and Fall*', *Folia Neohellenica* 4 (1982), 25–96.

[5] Cavafy, Ἀνέκδοτα σημειώματα ποιητικῆς καὶ ἠθικῆς (ed. G. P. Savidis, Athens 1983), p. 58.

II

This argument has been built on what is no more than a hint in 'Caesarion', and the charge of heavy-handedness is a ready one. But in any tradition the hints that lie in a poet's work are taken up and reworked by his successors. In the case of 'Caesarion' we shall find that Seferis, alert to hints, develops an aspect of the earlier poem in 'The King of Asine'. Another poet, Áris Aleksándru (1922–78) developed another point in his poem 'Meditations of Flavius Marcus' (1959): that by embedding Homer in a larger tradition Cavafy shows an understanding, as Eliot expressed it, of Homer's pastness as well as his presence: an understanding and an equilibrium peculiarly hard for the modern Greek poet to obtain.[6]

Of course you may translate verses of Homer.
This is an occupation legitimate, sometimes profitable;
at any rate it helps you to pass in the eyes of some
for a man of letters and – not without a certain note of condescension –
a connoisseur of poetry, *grosso modo* a poet.
Translate with zeal, albeit with care.
One thing alone is to be avoided.
Take care lest you translate into your life
the demeanour and the passions of the heroes
however much they seem to be your own
however certain you may be that you could have fallen before the walls of Troy.
Remember your belief your knowledge your conviction
that ultimately
on entering the city
you
would have found
smoke and ash.[7]

We are entitled to suspect that this is in a Cavafian spirit. The inadequacy of allusion to or translation from Homer is its inadequacy to the (implicit) circumstances of the present: in the years of

[6] Eliot, *Sacred Wood*, p. 49.

[7] Áris Aleksándru, «Φλάβιος Μάρκος εἰς ἑαυτόν», Ποιήματα (1941–1971) (Athens 1972), p. 128.

the 'cold civil war' which followed the Greek Civil War of 1946–9 the disquiet customarily felt by the more sensitive Greek poet about associating himself with Homer takes an acute form – especially because ancient Hellenism has been one of the pillars of right-wing regimes. It is interesting, in any case, to see how Cavafy, escaping from a sterile vein of romanticism, shows the way forward for other poets, even beyond Seferis.

PART FOUR
SEFERIS

*

Chapter Ten
Scholia

Generally Greek poets of the period of irredentism were content, in the vein of Valaoritis, to lay claim rather to the spirit of the Homeric heroes than to the letter of the Homeric poems. But the Asia Minor Disaster was a buffet to this way of thinking, and the failure of heroism was a subject explored by a number of influential novels in the decades that followed. The particular relevance of the issue to this study is that much of the impetus to making the Aegean coast of Turkey part of the Greek state derived from the fact that it had been the home of illustrious ancient Greek cities and perhaps of Homer's own: as Nikolareïzis indicated in 'The Presence of Homer in Modern Greek Poetry', the loss of Asia Minor was bound to change attitudes to Homer. There is an illuminating parallel with poetry in English. The generation of the English ruling class that went to the Great War constituted perhaps the widest reading public for Homer in Greek that there had ever been; and following the War it was an American poet resident in England who showed his revulsion against the whole enterprise in terms which overturned Homer:

> There died a myriad,
> And of the best, among them,
> For an old bitch gone in the teeth,
> For a botched civilization.

In this passage from *Hugh Selwyn Mauberley* Pound takes up the word Helen uses of herself in lamenting how she is the cause of the Trojan War: 'bitch' (*Iliad* 6.344); in doing so he alerts the reader to that side of Homer which is repelled by war, as opposed to that side which united young Englishmen and Germans in the feeling that to die in war was glorious: 'myriad' is not merely flowery for 'many' but the Homeric μύριοι.

The sack of the city of Smyrna by the Turks was perhaps the single most devastating incident of 1922, and it was Smyrna which perhaps most jealously clung to an ancient tradition that it was the birthplace of Homer. In more recent times it had been the home of strong irredentist feeling, exacerbated rather than diluted by the presence of a large non-Greek population and fuelled by the presence of the Evangelical School, which had a reputation for classical studies. The connection of the Great Idea and Homer in the public mind is depicted in the novel *In Hadzifrángu* (1963) by Kosmás Polítis (1888–1974):

> Mr Kurméndios rose: 'Stand up, and one minute's silence in honour of the glory of ancient Greece. In this theatre echoed the tragedies of Aeschylus and Sophocles. Here Homer Melesigenes sang his immortal epics.'[1]

In another novel by Politis, *Eroica* (1937), which is about a group of boys growing up in Smyrna, we find extended echoes of the *Iliad*: thanks to Pallis' new translation people actually live and breathe Homer and act out their lives in the light of the heroic way; Seferis too recalled Pallis' Homer as being formative.[2]

Of course Seferis stands out as a philologist among modern Greek poets, notable for his sustained study of the ancient texts, including Homer; and following the loss of his childhood home he turned for solace to the letter of Homer rather than to the nationalist mythology that had grown up around it.[3] Too many earlier Greek poets had tended to feel so sure of their position as heirs to Homer that it had not occurred to them, as Eliot put it, that tradition could not be inherited, and that if you wanted it you must obtain it by great labour.[4] To Seferis, by contrast, disinherited of his territorial birthright, the labour of acquainting himself with his literary birthright was something he had begun with some system well before reading Eliot's poetry or prose. And yet the first appearances of Homeric

[1] Kosmás Polítis, Στοῦ Χατζηφράγκου (Athens 1963), p. 59.

[2] Kosmas Politis, *Eroica* (ed. Peter Mackridge, Athens 1982); note editor's comments on pp. λθ′, μ′; compare Seferis, Δοκιμές vol. 1, p. 365.

[3] See generally Seferis, Μεταγραφές (ed. Y. Yatromanolákis, Athens 1980).

[4] Eliot, *Sacred Wood*, p. 49.

allusion in Seferis' work deliberately eschew claims to inheritance: they are oblique and ironic. Two tiny and fragmentary poems of 1926, '"Gloss" on the *Odyssey*' (about Circe) and 'Scholia' (on Calpyso) are exactly the opposite of what they purport to be: mythical women of the Homeric world are simply tongue-in-cheek references to personal love-lives of the present.[5] Dodging the question of the later poet's felt inferiority to Homer, Seferis not only disclaims the heroic mode associated with Homer's presence in modern Greece but dubs himself a mere commentator on the Homeric texts, thus disclaiming to be a poet at all.[6] In a manner of speaking, he does the same in the first of his collected poems which makes reference to Homer, 'The Companions in Hades' (1928):

fools, who devoured the oxen of Hyperion the Sun,
and he took away from them the day of their homecoming

Since we still had rusks
what witlessness it was
for us to eat on the shore
the Sun's slow-moving cattle

each one a castle
for you to besiege
for forty years, and set up for
a hero and a star!

We were hungry on the earth's back;
when we had eaten well
we fell here, low down,
clueless and sated.[7]

In this poem, especially as first printed, we find an affinity with a type of ancient epigram. Originally the poem had no title but was prefaced by the stage-direction, 'In Hades, the Companions of Odysseus are speaking': we may compare the note attached to an epigram in the *Palatine Anthology*, 'What Achilles would say on

[5] In Seferis, Μέρες vol. 1 (Athens 1975), p. 43 and Ἔξι νύχτες στὴν Ἀκρόπολη (Athens 1974), p. 52 respectively; see the discussion in Násos Vayenás, Ὁ ποιητὴς καὶ ὁ χορευτής. Μιὰ ἐξέταση τῆς ποιητικῆς καὶ τῆς ποίησης τοῦ Σεφέρη (Athens 1979), p. 170.

[6] Seferis, Ἔξι νύχτες, p. 51.

[7] Seferis, «Οἱ σύντροφοι στὸν Ἅδη», Ποιήματα (ed. G. P. Savidis, Athens 1982), p. 14.

seeing Odysseus in Hades'.[8] But there is in Seferis' poem also a touch of the ancient lyric poet Anacreon: compare the last lines of a poem on love and old age:

> For the recess of Hades
> is terrible, and painful
> the descent to it; and it is sure
> that who descends will not ascend.

A modern editor's comment on this is not unhelpful for 'The Companions in Hades': 'The only poem serious enough to find a place in Stobaeus' anthology ... The matter is solemn enough, but the metre is frivolous.'[9] 'The Companions' can be read – though it should not necessarily be read solely as this – as a gloss on the Asia Minor Disaster that in scale and tone is a rejection of an earlier generation's use of Homer.

Sikelianos' 'Homer', as we have seen, makes a hero of the successor poet by presenting him as a sort of reincarnation of Odysseus: here, by contrast, Seferis is taking an unusual step in having as his focus not the hero but his companions. Further, his epigraph cites the most severe judgement on them in the whole of the *Odyssey*, lines 8–9 of the proem.[10] In choosing this subject the poet creates for himself the *persona*, not of a Phemius – this, as we saw, was favoured by Palamas – but of a mere glossographer or scholiast on the forgotten men in Homer. It was Palamas himself, in an article of 1922, who connected the subversive rewritings of the *Odyssey* by the writers Nikos Kazantzakis and Nicolas Ségur (Episkopópulos) (1873–1944) with the turning upside down of the Greek world.[11] And in the light of this we may see the form of 'The Companions' as having a significance which goes beyond modernist experiments with the fragmentary and the marginal: the poet's dispassionate, even callous, attitude that we infer from the poem stands in stark contrast not only with the run of poems which mourn

[8] Seferis, Στροφή (Athens 1931), p. 16; *Anthologia Palatina* 9.459.

[9] Anacreon poem 395, with comment, in D. A. Campbell (ed.), *Greek Lyric Poetry* (London 1967).

[10] Maronitis, Ἡ ποίηση τοῦ Γιώργου Σεφέρη (Athens 1984), pp. 44–62; Ἀναζήτηση καὶ νόστος τοῦ Ὀδυσσέα (Athens 1982), pp. 72–6, 92–102.

[11] Palamas, Ἅπαντα vol. 12, pp. 349–51.

the loss of Homer's lands but also with a passage from one of the most interesting prose writers of the time, Fótis Kóndoglu (1897–1965), a native of Ayvalik. He describes spending August 1922 on the island of Lesbos off the coast of Asia Minor:

> All those who came from the other side told us that the Turks had not yet appeared, but from day to day they would come down to the sea. By day we saw smoke rising here and there, and by night fires all along the coast. Some were burning the sheaves on the threshing-floors because they could not take them with them; others were lighting fires and making signals to us, the wretches, seeking help, for they had no boats in which to leave. Often my eyes would fill with tears as I sat there on the sea-shore and looked across, while the sea roared between the Eastern land and the island where I was. Again and again there came into my mind these words which Homer says about the war at Troy:
>
> and all the time the piles of corpses burned thick and fast.[12]

The reference to Homer in this passage is moving because of its very incongruity: a single line recalled from a school set book is all that the narrator has to draw on by way of consolation (the line, *Iliad* 1.52, actually describes the piles of Greek dead killed by Apollo's plague). Seferis' poem, by contrast, is flippant; but it, too, reveals correspondences with Homer. Apart from the basic narrative feature, the eating of the Oxen of the Sun, we have specific analogies: 'rusks' for corn (*Odyssey* 12.327); 'witlessness' (κακοκεφαλιά) echoing 'evil insubordination' (ἀτασθαλίῃσι κακῇσι: 12.300); and 'the earth's back' formed on the basis of Homeric 'back of the sea' (νῶτα θαλάσσης: e.g. 3.142): finally, 'slow-moving cattle' (ἀργὰ γελάδια) is perhaps taken from the Homeric βόες ἀργοί (*Iliad* 23.30). These contribute to an unusual handling of the subject of 1922 which is nicely balanced between generality and specificity: 'we fell' (πέσαμε) could be 'fell in battle' or 'fell asleep', which makes us look beyond this particular set of circumstances to the laziness of the world's weaker brethren in general. In this poem,

[12] Fótis Kóndoglu, Ἔργα vol. 1 (Athens 1962), p. 241.

slight as it may be, there is a clearly new technique: the *Odyssey* and the Asia Minor Disaster, with the contrasting idioms of the epigraph and the poem, reflect against each other, and in doing so invert the expected appearance of Homer as a bolster of nationalism. This must have been quite shocking to readers when it first appeared.[13]

[13] Contrast e.g. N. E. Miliόris, Ἀπόηχοι τοῦ μικρασιατικοῦ ὀλέθρου στὴν ποίηση (Athens 1980), pp. 41, 44, 84.

Chapter Eleven
Ulysses/Disséas

I

UPON A FOREIGN VERSE

To Elli, Christmas 1931

Happy is he who has made the journey of Odysseus.
Happy if at the setting out he has felt sturdy a love's rigging spread through his body like the veins in which the blood hums.

Of a love with an indissoluble rhythm, unconquerable as music and eternal
because it was born when we were born, and as for whether it dies when we die, we do not know, and nor does anyone else.

I ask God to help me to say, at a moment of great bliss, what that love is;
I sit sometimes, surrounded by foreign parts, and I hear its distant hum like the sound of sea that has mingled with an inexplicable squall.

And there appears before me again and again the apparition of Odysseus, eyes red with the wave's salt
and the maturing desire to see once more the smoke emerging from the warmth of his house and his dog that has grown old waiting at the door.

He stands tall, whispering through his white beard words of our tongue as it was spoken three thousand years ago.
He extends a palm knotted by rope and tiller, with a skin worked by dry north wind, burning heat and snow.

You would say he was wanting to chase from among us the superhuman Cyclops who sees with a single eye, the Sirens that you hear and become forgetful, Scylla and Charybdis –
so many complicated monsters that prevent us from reflecting that he too was a man who struggled in the world, body and soul.

He is the great Odysseus, he who ordered the Wooden Horse to be built, and so the Achaeans won Troy.
I imagine that he is on his way to instruct me how to make a Wooden Horse so that I can win my own Troy.

For he speaks with humility and calmly, effortlessly, as if he knew me as a father,
or like some old seamen who, leaning on their nets at the time of storm and the winds' anger,

would tell me, in my childhood years, the song of Erotókritos, with tears in their eyes;
in those days when I used to be scared in my sleep on learning of the unjust fate of Aretí coming down the marble staircase.

He tells me of the difficulty and pain of feeling the sails of your ship swollen with memory and your soul's becoming the tiller.
And of your being alone, dark in the night and ungoverned like chaff on the threshing-floor.

Of the bitterness of seeing your companions sunk among the elements, scattered one by one.
And of how strangely you take courage from speaking with the dead when the living left to you are no longer enough.

He speaks – I still see his hands, that knew how to test whether the mermaid was well fitted to the prow,
granting me the waveless blue sea in the heart of winter.[1]

It has been said of this poem that its author was 'the first Greek to see the mythical Odysseus once again on a human scale'. A painting of 1935 by Kondoglu shows that this was not a uniquely Seferian way of seeing things: it depicts Odysseus and Ajax in a way which clearly models them on the modern folk – and in fact a detail from the picture was later reproduced in Kondoglu's collected writings with the title, 'Sailor lads of Ayvalik.'[2] Nothing could

[1] Seferis, «Πάνω σ' ἕναν ξένο στίχο», Ποιήματα, pp. 87–9.

[2] Savidis, Πάνω νερά, p. 16; for Kondoglu's painting see his Ἔργα vol. 1, p. 63 and the Wildenstein Gallery catalogue, *Theophilos*, *Kontoglou*, *Ghika*, *Tsarouchis: Four Painters of Twentieth-Century Greece* (London 1975), plate 20, and the dust-jacket of this book.

better illustrate the tension between the Ulysses of the Western classical tradition and the modern Greek Odisséas – or even Disseas – that is latent in modern Greece's relation to Homer and which Seferis memorably brings into the open in 'Upon a Foreign Verse'. The very title is designed to point out the tension: the verse referred to is 'foreign' both because it derives from Du Bellay's French (a language which Seferis knew very well but which was not his mother tongue) and, emotionally, because the speaking voice here is outside the Greek world and trying to establish access to it through what is to hand: a Western Ulysses. An early published version of the poem actually has as an epigraph the first words of Du Bellay's sonnet, 'Heureux qui, comme Ulysse ...'.[3] The sonnet celebrates the poet's love of his native Anjou over the classical grandeur of Rome: the Greek poet, ostensibly writing from London, and yearning for home, replaces the French poet's abstract Ulysses with an Odysseus of a recognizably modern Greek cast. The translation of Du Bellay's verse into a loosened political verse, with its folk associations, is an initial pointer to the character of Odysseus here; and it serves to distance the new poem from its predecessor. Seferis goes on in a cultivatedly discursive style to explore the figure of Odysseus.

II

Seferis' early novel, *Six Nights on the Acropolis*, which was published only posthumously, is an attempt to understand certain emotions through, among other devices, allusion to the *Odyssey*.[4] 'Upon a Foreign Verse' is a more disciplined and compressed version of the enterprise, with the poet asking in the first three couplets for the meaning of love (ἀγάπη) as a gloss on Du Bellay's 'Heureux' and receiving the answer in the remaining couplets with the figure of Odysseus. But it is not an incidental feature of the poem that it does not split cleanly into two parts. For the poet's reassurance is to lie in his part-identification with Odysseus; and the sixth verse, transitional between the two parts, forms the intersection of the

[3] Νέα Ἑστία no. 12 (Jul.–Dec. 1932), pp. 902–3.

[4] Seferis, Ἕξι νύχτες, e.g. pp. 52, 220, 223, 236–7.

evocative but vague imagery of the opening lines with the allusion to Homer which shapes the rest: 'I sit sometimes, surrounded by foreign parts'. The hero of *Six Nights on the Acropolis* declares of Homer at one point, in a phrase which reflects Seferis' own experience and outlook, 'sometimes I think that his poems are refugee poems'.[5] In 'Upon a Foreign Verse' Seferis articulates his feelings about absence from Greece through recollections of the seashore, not as his native shore, but as a place of exile and isolation. His feeling surrounded by exile re-enacts Odysseus' exile on Calypso's island (*Odyssey* 5.82–4):

> but he sat weeping on the shore, as before,
> rending his heart with tears and groans and pain.
> Shedding tears he gazed out over the unharvested sea.

The setting, then, prepares us for the appearance of Odysseus here; and this imagining oneself into the story has a precedent in 'Yannis Keats'. The salt-caked Odysseus is familiar from *Odyssey* 5.455–6:

> all his skin was swollen, and much sea was caked
> in his mouth and nose.

The smoke from the hero's house and the dog Argus are proverbial elements in the collective memory about Odysseus, but by subordinating them to the 'matured desire' (μεστωμένος, literally 'filled out' like fruit) Seferis brings out the importance of the seasons in the *Odyssey*. The date at the head of the poem is not, like the friend's name that stands with it, a mere vestige of the poem's occasion: it binds the poem into a seasonal pattern which gives it some coherence. Through the consolation of poetry the poet achieves an end to exile by moving the seasons, by making his own substitute for the divine ending of Odysseus' exile (*Odyssey* 1.16):

> but when the year came with the revolution of the seasons.

But Seferis, characteristically, finds solace not in the abstract but in the concrete: in setting out to describe the apparition of Odysseus

[5] Seferis, Ἔξι νύχτες, p. 53.

he is evidently reworking Sikelianos' 'Homer'. But the Odysseus with whom the Visionary identifies himself is proudly autochthonous – and the Wanderings are never mentioned in the cycle – while Seferis identifies himself as poet with Odysseus insofar as he is an exile. And his self-conscious aim to find Homer some role in his own poetry must indeed come to terms not only with Sikelianos but also with the disappearance of the whole irredentist climate which had made Sikelianos' recourse to Homer natural. As the classical scholar Sykutris, a native of Smyrna, put it in 1928:

> It is no coincidence that we have begun to pronounce the words 'Great Idea' with an ironical smile at the very period at which every schoolboy considers it his duty to his 'up-to-date' self to mock the 'scholastic' students of Demosthenes and Homer.[6]

It was not unnatural to lump together the classical past and the Great Idea as being jointly responsible for the disaster that had overcome Greece; and writers like Seferis' friend Yórgos Theotokás (1905–66) felt the need to speak up for a new Greek culture which would be free of any slavish dependence on the past. Theotokas' lively manifesto, *Free Spirit* (1929), signals the mood in its very title; but Seferis, for his part, always doubted whether freedom from the past was really liberating.[7] The tendency, after the 1922 collapse, to ignore Homer and the ancients as a stultifying influence was understandable; and yet Seferis continued to see Homer as a continuing source of solace and strength. Cavafy's interests now lay elsewhere; Palamas' *Nights of Phemius* are only tangentially related to Homer; Sikelianos had lost interest in Homer except as a small part of his mythological brew; Kariotakis makes no reference to Homer at all: Homeric allusion in modern Greek poetry survived 1922 because Seferis alone proved capable of fitting it to changed circumstances.

The fifth couplet indicates that the poet's felt intimacy with

[6] Sikutris, Μελέται καὶ ἄρθρα, p. 104.

[7] Yórgos Theotokás, Ἐλεύθερο πνεῦμα (ed. K. Th. Dimaras, Athens 1973); see also the correspondence between the two men: Theotokas and Seferis, Ἀλληλογραφία (1930–1966) (ed. G. P. Savidis, Athens 1975).

Odysseus is valued, above all, for the sound of the hero's voice: the language of the *Odyssey*, it is felt (wrongly, as it happens), was the spoken language of the time. The feeling fits the presentation of Odysseus here, not as a ruler who has suffered hardships through exceptional misfortune, but as a simple seafarer, a representative of the common people. There is in fact a particular figure behind the portrayal of Odysseus here; it is General Makriyannis, whose memoirs, published in 1907 from a semi-literate manuscript, were to leave a deep impression on Seferis both as a record of personal experience and as the most permanent embodiment of a popular style of thought and art which Seferis saw largely to have disappeared from Greece since. The hero of *Six Nights on the Acropolis* reads the *Odyssey* and the *Memoirs* of Makriyannis in parallel; writing of the General some years later Seferis states that 'If we really want to understand the ancients, we shall have always to study the soul of our common people.'[8] The question that arises with respect to 'Upon a Foreign Verse' is whether Seferis will be able to square Odysseus as mythical hero, Ulysses, with Odysseus as common man, Disseas.

The humanizing of Odysseus, so to speak, continues on a more abstract level in the following couplet with the recollection of these lines from Cavafy's 'Ithaca':

> The Laestrygonians and the Cyclopes,
> angry Poseidon, do not fear them;
> such things on your journey you will never find
> if your thought remains high, if a select
> emotion touches your spirit and body.
> The Laestrygonians and the Cyclopes,
> fierce Poseidon, you will never come across them,
> unless you carry them within your soul,
> unless your soul sets them up before you.

The dangers which beset Odysseus round are seen in 'Upon a Foreign Verse' frankly as monsters, the stuff of old wives' tales, complications which prevent real access to Odysseus – it sounds as if the poet is more or less restating the philosophy of 'Ithaca'. Yet,

[8] Seferis, Δοκιμές vol. 1, p. 257; Έξι νύχτες, p. 222.

while Cavafy's poem contains no named, let alone described, Odysseus, Seferis is anxious to convey the hero's physical presence.

The formal identification of Odysseus follows, echoing *Odyssey* 9.19–20:

> I am Odysseus son of Laertes, famous for my wiles
> among all men

and *Odyssey* 8.492–4:

> Come now, change your theme and sing of the setting up of the
> wooden horse,
> which Epeius made with the help of Athena,
> which on a time bright Odysseus took into the fortress as a ruse,
> filling it with men who sacked Ilion.

But there is now a pluralizing of Troys as with Cavafy's Ithacas: the poem is, if less abstractly than 'Ithaca', a didactic one. The core of the lesson that Odysseus has to give the present is that he 'speaks with humility and calmly'. This can be taken as an aesthetic and moral principle for the poet and compared to the famous lines from 'An Old Man on the River-Bank' (1942):

> I want nothing but to be able to speak simply, for this grace to
> be granted me.
> Because even our song we have laden with so much music that
> it is gradually sinking
> and our art we have adorned so much that its face has been eaten
> away by the gold
> and it is time for us to say our few words because our soul
> tomorrow sets sail.[9]

There is, to be sure, something arbitrary about taking bits from Seferis' poetry and reading them in this way, but a look at 'Upon a Foreign Verse' as a whole will justify a concentration on the phrase above. The word 'with humility' (ταπεινά) obviously fits the portrayal of Odysseus as one of the people, beyond being a term of approbation; further, 'effortlessly' fits as much the flowing demotic of Makriyannis' prose as the words of Odysseus falling thick as snow (*Iliad* 3.222); finally, γαλήνη, meaning a calm sea and hence

[9] Seferis, «Ἕνας γέροντας στὴν ἀκροποταμιά», Ποιήματα, p. 201.

a calm temperament, is appropriate to describe the mood of a seaman. The poet's intention is clear: to find and describe in the figure of Odysseus those characteristics of an older and better world which we now seem to have lost.

It is no surprise to find such a world being identified with that of Seferis' childhood in the lines that follow; and the detail of the recital of the romance *Erotókritos* by the sailors is not just a bit of local colour or the intrusion of a preoccupation of the poet's: it is central to the poem.[10] The mention of *Erotokritos* here does not constitute mere escapism into a world of childhood: it is a means of reassessing tactfully the modern Greek poet's relation to Homer. Like Makriyannis, *Erotokritos* is a central text of the 'Greek tradition' as understood by Seferis; in particular, it is for Seferis just as much a 'refugee poem' as Homer's, as a work which was particularly popular in Seferis' lost land of Asia Minor. The appearance of the Renaissance romance here in place of the ancient epic shows that the poet – in marked and deliberate contrast to Sikelianos – is delicately holding back from direct claims to Homeric inspiration while implicitly rooting Homer in his native Asia Minor as opposed to Du Bellay's West.

The next couplet returns us to the journey of Odysseus as related by himself, a journey seen as a spiritual test. This might sound too abstract, a rather forced, if venerable, moral interpretation of the *Odyssey*, were it not tied into a web of allusion to other poetry. In the first place, the phrase 'like chaff on the threshing-floor', taken from folk song, recalls the season of Odysseus' journey from Calypso's island, when his raft is buffeted by the winds (*Odyssey* 5.328–30):

> as when the north wind in autumn carries thistles
> over the plain, and they cling close to one another,
> so the winds bore [the raft] here and there over the sea.[11]

The couplet also hints at the episode of Palinurus in the *Aeneid*. Although Aeneas' helmsman there is the victim of Lethe rather than

[10] Seferis, Δοκιμές vol. 1, p. 12; Μέρες vol. 2 (Athens 1975), p. 20.
[11] The line of folk song in Seferis, Δοκιμές vol. 1, p. 260.

of uncontrolled memory, Odysseus' lone helmsmanship in 'Upon a Foreign Verse' puts him in the subsequent position of Aeneas (5.867–9):

> When the father [Aeneas] felt the ship floating with its master lost,
> he himself took charge of the craft in the night waves,
> with many a groan, and stunned at heart for the loss of his friend.

It is not hard to see how an Asia Minor Greek after 1922 will, ironically enough, feel a special affinity to the Trojan's plight – and Seferis' Homer, as we shall see, is one very much bound up with later literature.[12]

III

The next couplet, like 'The Companions in Hades', points us to the *Odyssey*'s proem; but its second line sits rather uncomfortably with the first, and exposes a central weakness in the poem: it is the point at which 'Upon a Foreign Verse', which has so far easily and evocatively blended ancient and modern, breaks apart. Odysseus' descent to the Underworld is in the epic understood as being for a clear purpose, to ask Tiresias how to get home: it is not understood – surprisingly, perhaps – as in any overt sense a rite of passage. When Seferis writes

> And of how strangely you take courage from speaking with the dead when the living left to you are no longer enough

he seems to be foisting his thoughts about senior living poets into the reported speech of Odysseus, which at this point draws to a close. The verse, describing as it does the poet's own sense of the renewed strength derived from speaking with the apparition of Odysseus, leads neatly back to his own concluding thoughts – but it appears too nakedly exploitative of the figure of Odysseus as a source of inspiration not vouchsafed to other poets. The word ἀντρειεύομαι, indeed, which I have translated as 'take courage' has connotations of gaining in virility which are alien to the Odyssean

[12] See here the statement by the poet in Μέρες vol. 5, p. 169.

descent to the Underworld and closer to those of Pound's Canto I, where we find the phrase, 'strong with the blood'.

The question of the relation of 'Upon a Foreign Verse' to contemporary poets is particularly germane because Seferis has not in fact produced a mode of recourse to Homer which is genuinely distinctive: we can see this by comparing a passage from Kazantzakis' tragedy *Odysseus* (1922–3), whether or not Seferis had read it:

> By the light of a lightning-bolt I spy of a sudden
> Odysseus in the middle of the sea
> calmly holding the rudder tight,
> facing right into the squall!
> 'Odysseus', I call to him, 'are you off home?
> Was the Goddess' bed no longer room enough for you?'
> But he, with tiller in hand,
> biting his salty moustache,
> looked on ahead, hunched, and did not turn my way![13]

It is precisely in Seferis' rejection of the living that we discern his failure to escape the living. The general affinity with Odysseus as exile is persuasive only insofar as it forgets Odysseus' penchant for telling false stories – in Kazantzakis' play, indeed, the above passage is in the mouth of the mendacious hero himself.

For Seferis the figure of Odysseus grants the exiled poet spiritual calm, and the Greek poet abroad is sustained by a synthesis of ancient and modern. But the overriding importance of the Homeric poems themselves is not evident; and the attribution of the poet's feeling of creative strength to the humble seafaring Odysseus is less than convincing. It is, as we shall see, in the final poem of the collection *Mythistorema* that Seferis will create a new type of *Nekyia* and with it a new and distinctive way of drawing on Homer that is unhampered by the tension between a Ulysses of literature and a Disseas of life.

[13] Kazantzakis, Ὀδυσσέας (Athens 1928), p. 37.

Chapter Twelve
Homer and the poetic vocation

I

Here end the sea's works, love's works.
Those who will one day live where we come to an end,
if it chance that the blood blacken in their memories and
overflow,
let them not forget us, the weak souls among the asphodels,
let them turn towards Erebus the victims' heads:

We who had nothing will teach them calm.[1]

Seferis' collection *Mythistorema* (1935) is perhaps the most influential single work of poetry in twentieth-century Greece, and certainly the work most famously associated with Homeric myth; it has also inspired an ample critical literature.[2] What I have to say here may provoke dissent not so much for what it says – this, I hope, rests on firm ground – as for what it omits. For my title indicates that the discussion here will be confined to the last poem of the collection, quoted above. How can this be justified?

The first thing to affirm is that the concern of this book is with the possibilities for and achievements in the short poem in modern Greek, and not with Homer's significance, psychological or otherwise, for any whole *œuvre*: the indiscriminate search, say, for *all* Homeric elements in the work of Seferis often becomes a distraction.[3] My aim is to examine certain individual poems in which Homeric allusion is a central shaping force rather than to accumulate more or less casual references. Furthermore, *Mythistorema*, as I said above, is to be seen as much as a collection as a unitary work; this neglected point needs some developing with reference to the collection's title. *Mythistorema* means in the ordinary way *Novel*; but Seferis was keen to mine the word for its palpable components,

[1] Seferis, Ποιήματα, p. 71.

[2] See Dimítris Daskalópulos, Ἐργογραφία τοῦ Σεφέρη (Athens 1979).

[3] For possible Homeric echoes in the collection as a whole see Ricks, 'Homer and Greek Poetry', pp. 173–200.

mythos and *historia*.[4] In some ways the poet's choice of title has proved to be a mixed blessing. In the first place, critics have tended to dwell too closely on history narrowly interpreted as the Asia Minor Disaster; secondly, ancient mythical elements have become the object, as a recent assessment notes, of 'scholarly if not always critical attention'; above all, criticism has been mesmerized by Eliot's term, 'the mythical method'.[5] But it is very forced to maintain of *Mythistorema* what Eliot observes of *Ulysses* in his famous review, that it maintains 'a continuous parallel between contemporaneity and antiquity'. Joyce's novel, broadly speaking, keeps a one-to-one connection between its chapters and episodes in the *Odyssey*; but the poems of *Mythistorema*, by contrast, though numbered 1–24 (Α′–ΚΔ′), cannot be correlated with the *Odyssey*'s Books 1–24 (α–ω).[6] What we have in Seferis' cycle, by and large – take for example the poem headed 'Astyanax' – are Homeric resonances rather than Homeric correspondences – and a crucial and neglected fact about *Mythistorema* is that it was first published without numbering as a collection of short untitled poems. I have the suspicion myself that the title *Novel* was chosen teasingly to set the work with and against the Thirties novel in Greece – and especially the novel *Argo* by Seferis' friend Theotokas (first volume 1933). The suspicion is borne out by the comment of the French Neohellenist Louis Roussel, who translated the collection as *Roman* but wrote, 'This Novel is nothing other than verses.'[7] There is, finally, some debate about how 'mythical' *Mythistorema* actually is anyway, if by that we mean that it alludes in a specific and sustained way to ancient Greek texts. The doubts that one may have about this critical *idée fixe* find a good parallel with today's scepticism

[4] See the note by the poet which originally stood at the front of *Mythistorema*, Ποιήματα, p. 314.

[5] Savidis, 'The Tragic Vision of George Seferis', *Grand Street* 5.2 (Winter 1986), 153–74; quotation from p. 156. For the 'mythical method', with some afterthoughts, see Edmund Keeley, *Modern Greek Poetry. Voice and Myth* (Princeton 1983), pp. 75–6.

[6] Eliot, 'Ulysses, Order and Myth' (1923), in *Selected Prose* (ed. Frank Kermode, New York 1975), 175–8. An attempt to correlate *Mythistorema* with the *Odyssey* has been made by Ruth Padel, 'Homer's Reader: a Reading of George Seferis', *Proceedings of the Cambridge Philological Society* 211 (n.s. 31) (1985), 74–132.

[7] Louis Roussel quoted in Daskalopulos, Ἐργογραφία Σεφέρη, p. 36; see also Roderick Beaton, 'Myth and Text: Readings in the Modern Greek Novel', *Byzantine and Modern Greek Studies* 9 (1984–5), 29–53.

about Stuart Gilbert's painstaking book on *Ulysses*.[8] And it is also to be noted that those who place greatest weight on the importance of Greek myth for Seferis are normally those who are not themselves Greek and are therefore less able to observe those sides of Seferis' work which do not derive from a shared Western culture.

This new look at the final poem of *Mythistorema*, then, claims to be anything but a 'key' to the cycle as a whole. But it does examine a central preoccupation of Seferis' poetry and the centrality of Homer to that preoccupation: the *Nekyia*. The revival of this episode from the *Odyssey*, and its endowment with a new significance for the present, is perhaps Seferis' most distinctive contribution to European poetry.

In the *Odyssey* the hero narrates to the Phaeacians how he was instructed by Circe to go down to Hades in order to consult the seer Tiresias about his journey home. On reaching the Underworld, Circe instructs Odysseus (10.516–40):

> Here then, hero, with firm tread, as I tell you,
> dig a cavity a cubit square;
> pour libations round it to all the dead:
> first milk and honey, then sweet wine,
> and lastly water, with a scattering of white barley.
> Then do full obeisance to the strengthless heads of the dead:
> that on arrival at Ithaca you will sacrifice your finest heifer,
> and make a great fire in the halls, and fill it with good things
> and sacrifice to Tiresias individually a black
> lamb, excellent among all your flock.
> But when you have appeased the glorious nations of the dead
> sacrifice a ram and a black ewe,
> turning them towards Erebus; but yourself turn your head away
> towards the streams of the river; from there shall many
> souls of the dead come forth.
> Then you must order and bid your companions
> to flay and burn those sheep which lie
> slaughtered by the pitiless bronze and pray to the gods,
> mighty Hades and worthy Persephone;

8 Stuart Gilbert, *James Joyce's Ulysses: a Study* (New York 1930). On the question of myth and *Mythistorema* see Keeley, *Modern Greek Poetry*, pp. 86–94, a response to Vayenas, Ὁ ποιητὴς καὶ ὁ χορευτής, pp. 150–5.

but you, draw your sword from your hip
and crouch down, and do not allow the strengthless heads of the dead
to approach the blood before you see Tiresias.
Then, chief of men, he will come to you as a seer
and will tell you your way and the distance of your journey
and the homecoming you will travel over the fishy sea.

The penultimate line of Seferis' poem is a clear reference to the above source: 'let them turn towards Erebus the victims' heads'. What is seen to be particularly significant about this passage? Up to this point in *Mythistorema* everything – and the *Nekyia* anticipated in the ninth poem is no exception – has been teasingly unresolved, culminating in the penultimate poem:

A little further
we shall see the almond-trees in flower
marble gleaming in the sun
the sea breaking into waves

a little further,
let us rise a little higher.[9]

In the final poem too there is a muted hope for the future – but what, if anything, does this have to do with Homer?

It is evident that Seferis has inverted the situation of the Homeric *Nekyia*: the dead appear to take the initiative in speaking to the living, and the scene is viewed from their angle. But the later poet preserves the flow of blood as the agent of connection between the living and the dead; and he does so by conflating the relevant phrase from the *Odyssey* (11.36), 'the black blood flowed' with a completely unrelated passage from the *Iliad*. During his quarrel with Achilles at the start of the poem (1.103) Agamemnon is overcome with anger, which the poet understands physiologically as being a flow of blood to the midriff, the seat of the emotions, so that it turns black inside. Seferis, then, is proposing an antidote to anger and suffering: to let the blood flow so that it may attract the dead, who may have the power to teach future generations a better way. The

[9] Seferis, Ποιήματα, pp. 54, 70.

message is heightened by two further Homeric reminiscences which point a contrast between Achilles and the collective voice of Seferis' poem. In the first place we have the dead 'among the asphodels'. Homer shows Achilles, a lord even among the dead, striding across the asphodel meadow (*Odyssey* 11.539) – a picture revived by Sikelianos – while for Seferis there are among the asphodels but 'weak souls'. We may take this as a moralizing of the Homeric 'strengthless heads': Seferis' speakers, though ostensibly weak like 'The Companions in Hades', can still be of use to future generations. They will not return to the Upper World with avenging force, like the Achilles of Sikelianos' 'Secret Iliad', which, as we have seen, rejects the *Nekyia* of the *Odyssey* as of no consequence: they will remain in Hades, weak in themselves but still exerting, or hoping to exert, some influence in the world above. Now it is my proposal that through this poem Seferis is modestly asserting the value of the poet's vocation. In order to see how and why, we must turn aside from Homer at this point and look at an unlikely trio of authors: Marcus Aurelius, Ezra Pound and Kostas Kariotakis.

II

Perhaps the sole momentary note of certainty struck in the whole of *Mythistorema* is in the concluding words of the opening poem:

> Φέραμε πίσω
> αὐτὰ τ' ἀνάγλυφα μιᾶς τέχνης ταπεινῆς
>
> ('*We brought back these carved reliefs of a humble art/craft*').

Are we to see in these lines a self-conscious preoccupation with the poet's calling? Are the sculptures to be understood as being the sequence of little poems that follow? An allusion in these lines to another modern Greek poet makes the inference plausible; the poem in question, whose very subject is poetry itself, is the 'March Funereal and Vertical' (1927) by Kariotakis:

> I see the plasterwork on the ceiling.
> Maeanders draw me into their dance.
> My happiness, I am thinking, must be
> a matter of height.

Symbols of a higher life,
roses unchanging, transubstantiated
white thorns all around
an Amaltheian horn.

(Humble art without style,
how late in the day do I accept your teaching!)
Dream relief, I shall approach you
vertically.

Horizons will have smothered me.
In all climates, at all latitudes,
struggles for bread and salt,
love-affairs, boredom.

Oh yes, now I must wear
that handsome plaster crown.
With the ceiling framing me like that,
I shall look very well.[10]

Picking on the words ταπεινὴ τέχνη and ἀνάγλυφα here, we are entitled to infer that Seferis' use of the same words is itself programmatic; that the sculptures are humble because they renounce the heroic sublime (ὕψος) of the generation of Sikelianos. But the relationship with Kariotakis deserves a little more attention.

Kariotakis was still arguably the most influential Greek poet when Seferis published *Mythistorema*: he had the undeniable attraction of being dead – better, a suicide. (The poem quoted above is one of many in which suicide is endorsed.) He even had an '-ism' named after him: καρυωτακισμός was a vein of maudlin pessimism, as practised by its less talented exponents, which infected a whole generation of poets. But Kariotakis' work held no acknowledged attraction for Seferis; for his method was to write in the regular metres and stanza-forms used by his contemporaries but to disrupt their rhythms and diction by lacing them with journalese, the purist idiom of bureaucracy, and so on; and this was frowned on by one of demoticist upbringing such as Seferis. The greatest point of difference between Seferis and his senior, however, is that the latter

[10] Kariotakis, « Ἐμβατήριο πένθιμο καὶ κατακόρυφο », Ποιήματα, p. 113; for Seferis' allusion, see G. P. Savidis' introduction, p. λθ'.

eschewed allusions to ancient myth. It is not surprising, accordingly, that the name of Kariotakis is scarcely to be found in Seferis' essays; nor is it surprising, on the other hand, that Seferis was unable to escape the influence of Kariotakis altogether. This holds not just for the opening poem of *Mythistorema* but for its closing poem, as the following quotation from Kariotakis will show:

TOMBS

Eléni S. Lámari 1878–1912
Poetess and musician.
She died in the most terrible physical pain
and with the greatest spiritual calm.

How great the peace that reigns here!
The very tombs seem to be smiling,
while the dead, deep in the darkness below,
speak quietly in capital letters.

From there to our hearts which are at peace
they wish to ascend with simple words.
But their complaints, or whatever they may say,
are of no use – so far away have they gone.

Look there: Martzókis is now but two
crossed bits of wood. Here is Vasiliadis too,
a large stone book.

And a tombstone half-hidden in greenery
– Hades' way of symbolizing her now –
there is Lamari, forgotten poetess.[11]

A good many of Kariotakis' poems are about poetry itself – a feature which, in less able hands, has proved an undesirable legacy for Greek poetry – and this is one reason why, if the opening poem of *Mythistorema* is indeed programmatic, it can hardly steer clear of Kariotakis altogether. In 'Tombs' (1927) Kariotakis uses the idea of souls speaking from the darkness of the Underworld, but he makes it almost completely un-mythical in its associations, first by identifying the speech of the dead with the words carved on modern

[11] Kariotakis, «Τάφοι», Ποιήματα, p. 91.

tombstones, and secondly by taking as his examples two minor ninteenth-century poets and an obscure poetess; in addition, he replaces the specific Homeric Ἔρεβος with the vaguer plural ἐρέβη, meaning the darkness below without an indication of its location.[12] It is possible to infer from these features that Seferis' return to the text of the *Odyssey* itself is an attempt to upstage Kariotakis and to affirm for his own case the possibility of enduring fame which Kariotakis denies the woman mentioned.

But, while the revival of the Odyssean *Nekyia* is characteristically Seferian, it is not Seferis' discovery alone: there is a telling, and strangely neglected, parallel with Pound.[13] Pound's first Canto, bar its last five lines, consists of this episode from the *Odyssey*: the passage begins with the famous lines, 'And then went down to the ship ...' and goes on with a free paraphrase of the section of Book 11. Why did Pound begin his long work with the Homeric *Nekyia*? To say that Joyce's *Ulysses* alone explains the decision is an over-simplification: Pound had been working on the idea of the *Cantos* since the first decade of the century; and the decision to begin with this episode is the reformulation of a programmatic intent which had equally been there in the opening sentence of the first Canto as published in *Poetry* in 1917 – the *Nekyia* was then in the third Canto – and stated with exasperated bravado:

> Hang it all, there can be but one *Sordello*!
> But say I want to, say I take your whole bag of tricks,
> Let in your quirks and tweeks, and say the thing's an art-form,
> Your *Sordello*, and that the modern world
> Needs such a rag-bag to stuff all its thought in,
> Say that I dump my catch, shiny and silvery
> As fresh sardines flapping and slipping on the marginal
> cobbles?[14]

[12] For ἐρέβη in an unspecific sense, a sense, at least, not closely connected with ancient myth, see e.g. Seferis' poem «Ρίμα» (Ποιήματα, p. 23) or Yánnis Rítsos' poem «Ἀνικανοποίητος», Ποιήματα 1930–1960 vol. 1 (Athens 1972), p. 32.

[13] We cannot rule out the possibility of influence or imitation: Seferis published translations of 'Exile's Letter' (*Cathay*) in 1935 and of Canto I in 1939 (Seferis, Ἀντιγραφές (Athens 1963), pp. 52–61).

[14] Here as reprinted in Ronald Bush, *The Genesis of Ezra Pound's Cantos* (Princeton 1976), p. 53.

Pound reiterates in his critical work that of the Victorians it is only Browning who has left a live form – and it is in this connection that his recourse to Homer is to be understood: 'My pawing over the ancients and semi-ancients has been one long struggle to find out what has been done, once for all, better than it can ever be done again, and to find out what remains for us to do.'[15] By 1925 Pound had, perhaps wisely, decided to attempt a less overt reckoning with Browning, who is relegated to the beginning of the new Canto II. How does his drawing on Homer serve his purpose?

The first point to be made is that Pound is consciously reaching back to what he believes, rightly or wrongly, to be the oldest part of Homer and hence the oldest part of European poetry: 'The Nekuia shouts aloud that it is *older* than the rest... hinter-time.'[16] In a search for new resources of expression, Pound overleaps Browning to reach the oldest poetic monument. The second point is that Pound has taken Homer not in the original Greek but in the Latin translation of Andreas Divus Justinopolitanus (1538). This is not out of sheer ignorance or eccentricity: it is integral to the overall purpose. Turning to Andreas Divus' Latin crib helps Pound to escape the idiom of Victorian and Edwardian Hellenism, and, beyond this, provides an ancestral voice less distinguished than Homer's own – one which Pound can address like this:

> Lie quiet, Divus, I mean, that is Andreas Divus,
> in officina Wecheli, 1538, out of Homer.[17]

In the act of feeling his way back through the voices of Andreas and Homer, Pound is clearing a place for his own – an ambitious but achieved gesture. In his attempt to go beyond Browning, Pound turns to Homer: so too does Seferis, pitting himself against Kariotakis.

III

I have pointed to Kariotakis as an influence Seferis is trying to escape, and to Pound as a near-contemporary parallel. But Seferis

[15] Pound, *Literary Essays*, p. 11; on Browning see p. 33.
[16] Pound, *Selected Letters* (ed. D. D. Paige, London 1971), p. 274.
[17] Pound, *Cantos* (London 1975), p. 5; see also 'Early Translators of Homer', *Literary Essays*, pp. 249–75.

had to deal, not just with his anxieties as a new poet, but with a more far-reaching anxiety as to whether poetry was possible at all. Such thoughts were in his mind during the writing of *Mythistorema*, as we can see from an ancient observation which he translated in 1934: 'How many of those who were once hymned are now consigned to oblivion; and how many of those who hymned them have long been lost.' The sentence comes from the *Meditations* of Marcus Aurelius (7.6).[18] It is not surprising that Seferis should have been reading this famous work; but it is remarkable, and we see it from the markings on his own copy of the *Meditations*, how he dwells on those passages of the philosopher-king which hit at the poet, to whom posthumous fame is everything. Seferis notes this passage, for example:

> Each man, then, lives but this short time, and small is the little corner of the earth on which he lives; small too is the most far-reaching posthumous fame which itself follows a succession of homunculi who will soon die and who know not even themselves, let alone one long dead. (3.10)

And this:

> Of human life the duration is a moment; the substance in flux; the sense dim; the physical constitution perishable; the soul a delirium; the fortune hard to establish; the fame a matter of indifference. In short, everything of the body is a river; everything of the soul is a dream and a fever; life is a war and the sojourn of a visitor; posthumous fame is to be forgotten. What then can send us on our way? One thing and one alone: philosophy. (2.17)

Marcus' outlook is a bleak one, and the reason why Seferis noted it is that it has particularly unwelcome consequences for the poet. And it is interesting that the very thing to which Seferis turns in order to attempt the escape from doubts about the purpose of poetry is one that Marcus happens to hold up to especial scorn: he observes of some absurd beliefs that 'even the episode of the *Nekyia* seems more probable!' (9.24). Seferis, anxious to justify the place of the *Nekyia* as something of enduring meaning and value, demands as a

[18] For Seferis' translation see Μεταγραφές, p. 195; generally, see the editorial material on pp. 309–16.

poet both an after-life in the collective memory and access to the wisdom of past generations. In making this demand he is engaged in the substitution of poetry for philosophy in Marcus' declaration above: the ancient quarrel between poetry and philosophy is being waged. But the preoccupation with the question of 'posthumous fame' (ὑστεροφημία), a word which Seferis noted down from his reading of Marcus, takes us back to Kariotakis. If all human life is in flux, then allusion, by which a poet marks out, more or less consciously, what he considers to be most important in that past, is useless; and the poet's attempt to bridge the gap between himself and future generations is futile. But we find that it is the very word ὑστεροφημία that is the title of the opening poem of Kariotakis' last collection (1927):

POSTHUMOUS FAME

Our death is required by boundless nature all around
and the flowers' purple mouths demand it.
If spring comes again it will once again desert us
and from then on we shall not be even shadows of shadows.

Our death is awaited by the sun's bright light.
One more triumphant sunset like this we shall see,
and then we shall be leaving April evenings
on our way to the dark kingdoms beyond.

All that can be left after us is our verses,
just ten of our verses left, as when
shipwrecked sailors scatter doves to chance,
and when the message is brought it is too late.[19]

The final poem of *Mythistorema* is itself like a scattering of doves, an attempt to reach beyond what is available in the present. Such enterprises Marcus Aurelius renounces and even condemns – and yet, if Marcus had been as good as his word, would we still read him so many centuries on? Matthew Arnold pondered in his concluding remark about the philosopher-king,

What would have become of his notions of the *exitiabilis superstitio*, of the 'obstinacy of the Christians'? Vain ques-

[19] Kariotakis, «Ὑστεροφημία», Ποιήματα, p. 63.

tion! yet the greatest charm of Marcus Aurelius is that he makes us ask it. We see him wise, just, self-governed, thankful, blameless; yet, with all this, agitated, stretching out his arms for something beyond, – *tendentemque manus ripae ulterioris amore.*[20]

In this peroration Arnold adapts a famous line from Virgil (*Aeneid* 6.314), who describes the shades in the Underworld, unable to cross the river Cocytus:

tendebantque manus ripae ulterioris amore

('*and they stretched out their arms in longing for the opposite shore*').

Seferis himself was gripped by this line and adapted it in his poem, 'An Old Man by the River-Bank':

καὶ τὸ χάσμα τῆς πρόσκλησης τῶν συντρόφων ἀπὸ τὸν ἀντίπερα γιαλό

('*and the gap between us and the calling of our companions on the opposite shore*').[21]

But what is to be noted above all is that Arnold's way of ending an essay with a quotation, or Seferis' of quoting it in a new poem, show the hold of poetry on the collective memory. It was, accordingly, not only characteristic of, but fitting for, Seferis to end the *Mythistorema* collection with a word taken from the Homeric *Nekyia*, ἔρεβος. In doing so – and we recall the end of Foscolo's 'Dei Sepolcri' – Seferis establishes a place for poetry in general and for poetry of his own.

[20] Arnold, *Essays Literary and Critical*, p. 209.
[21] Seferis, Ποίηματα, p. 200.

Chapter Thirteen
Beyond the folk tradition

I

THE EXILE'S RETURN

– Old friend, what are you in search of?
After years of exile you have arrived
with images that you have nurtured
under foreign skies
far from your own country.

– I am in search of my old garden;
the trees come up to my waist
and the hills look like terraces,
and yet when I was a boy
I used to play on the grass
under the great shadows
and run on the slopes
for hours on end out of breath.

– Old friend, relax
little by little you will get used to things;
we shall go together up the paths you know,
we shall rest together
under the plane-trees' dome,
bit by bit your garden and your slopes
will come to you.

– I am in search of my old house
with the tall windows
obscured by ivy,
I am in search of the ancient column
that the seaman looked upon.
How, I ask, can I enter this fold?
The roof comes up to my shoulders,
and as far as I can see
I see people kneeling
as if saying their prayers.

– Old friend, can't you hear me?
Little by little you will get used to things,
your house is the one that you can see,
and on this door your friends and people
will shortly be knocking
to give you a sweet welcome home.

– Why is your voice far away?
Lift your head a little
so that I can catch what you are saying to me,
as you speak your stature
is ever dwindling
as if you are sinking into the ground.

– Old friend, use your head,
little by little you will get used to things,
your nostalgia has created
a non-existent land, with laws
beyond the earth and men.

– I now no longer hear a thing,
my last friend has sunk,
strange how everything about
is lowered every so often;
over here cross, harvesting,
thousands of chariots with scythed wheels.

Athens, spring '38.[1]

The title of Seferis' poem is the one customarily given to one of the best-known Greek ballads, the basic elements of which are these: a man meets a woman, and after getting into conversation reveals that he is her long-lost husband; she demands proof of this, and a version of the following dialogue takes place:

– Stranger, if you are my husband, if you are my good man,
show me marks of the yard and then I shall believe you.
– You have an apple-tree at your door and a vine in your yard;
it makes rosé grapes and muscat wine,
and whoever drinks it is refreshed and asks for more.

[1] Seferis, «῾Ο γυρισμὸς τοῦ ξενιτεμένου», Ποιήματα, pp. 163–5.

– These are marks of the yard, the whole world knows them;
you were passing by, you went by, you saw them, and you tell me.
Tell me marks of the house and then I shall believe you.
– In the middle of the chamber a golden candle is alight,
and it shines on you as you undress and plait your hair;
it shines on you at sweet dawn when you put on your best clothes.
– Some wicked neighbour told you this and you know it.
Tell me marks of the body, marks of love.
– You have a mole on your breast and a mole under your arm,
and between your two breasts your husband's amulet.
– Stranger, you are my husband, you are my good man.[2]

Now what has this to do with Homer? Somewhat surprisingly, no critic has yet thought of drawing together Homer and the folk tradition in a study of the poem; though D. N. Maronitis acknowledges that in the seaman here we have a type of Odysseus.[3] Without attempting to elbow out the cogent interpretation of the folklore elements in the poem that has been advanced by Maronitis, I shall devote attention here to a connection with the Homeric poems as giving a further resonance to 'The Exile's Return'. Specifically, the poem can be read as following the path of the second half of the *Odyssey*, but with the happy ending twisted so that we return to the moment of greatest despair in the wanderings of Odysseus, the eating of the Oxen of the Sun (alluded to in 'The Companions in Hades') and beyond that to the events of the *Iliad*. Let us see how this pattern unfolds through a reading of the poem in which, as much to avoid assumptions as for brevity, the two interlocutors are referred to as *A* and *B*.

The first section of the poem can be understood as a reworking of the central break in the *Odyssey* (13.187–9), when the sleeping Odysseus is deposited safely in Ithaca by the Phaeacians:

and bright Odysseus awoke
from sleep in his native land, but he did not recognize it,
having been away for a long time.

[2] N. G. Politis, Ἐκλογαί, pp. 120–2.

[3] Maronitis, Σεφέρης, pp. 29–43 and 148n; I am indebted to this discussion.

B, like Odysseus, has been long absent from his country – as Seferis had been in the Thirties – and *A*'s question is by what signs he will recognize it. The section that follows can in turn be seen as a reflection of two further passages related to Odysseus' homecoming. The first comes from Book 24 (336–8), the point at which Odysseus identifies himself to his father Laertes after a seemingly cruel and pointless charade of deception:

> Come now, I shall tell you about the trees in the well-constructed terrace
> that once you gave me, and I used to ask you about each one
> when I was a little boy, going about the garden.

A first worrying sign appears in the corresponding part of Seferis' poem: the trees appear not bigger, as we should expect, but smaller, casting doubt on the authenticity of the homeland. This takes us back to the passage cited earlier, in which Odysseus is still unaware that he is back in Ithaca (Athena has cast a mist over the island); it contains a number of topographical features analogous to those found in the second and third sections of Seferis' 'Return':

> and so to the lord everything appeared different:
> the extending paths and the harbours capacious of ships
> and the sheer rocks and the spreading trees. (13.194–6)

By the importation of a sense of difference into the context of the garden, Seferis makes the end of the *Odyssey*, as much as the middle, a moment of bewilderment.

In the third section, *A*'s injunction to *B* indicates *B*'s disturbed state of mind, comparable to that of Odysseus at *Odyssey* 13.219–21:

> and he lamented his homeland,
> dragging his way along the shore of the roaring sea
> with great lamentation

and *A*'s claim that *B* will get used to things runs parallel to the advice that Athena gives Odysseus later in Book 13 (306–10):

> I shall tell you what ills shall be your lot to suffer
> in the well-built house; but you must endure them through necessity

and not tell anyone, man or woman,
that you have arrived on your wanderings, but endure
many ills in silence, putting up with violence at men's hands.

There is a great weight of sinister thoughts behind the words of *A*, to be sure; and note too that while in the *Odyssey* we are clear about Athena's good will, we are here far from clear about – and perhaps already suspicious of – *A*'s motives. It is as if in 'The Return' we are infected with Odysseus' initial suspicion of Athena (13.324–8):

but now I supplicate you in the name of your father – for I think
that I have not arrived in bright Ithaca, but am roaming over
some other
land; and I think that you are saying this
to tease me, in order to deceive my wits –
tell me if I really have arrived at my own country.

In the fourth section the locus of recognition sought by *B* is now his house itself: there is a narrowing of focus which follows not only the plot of the *Odyssey* (the island Ithaca; the outer part of the estate, the home of the swineherd Eumaeus; the house of Odysseus; the marital bedchamber of Odysseus and Penelope) but also the sequence of 'marks' of the 'Return' ballad (the yard; the wife's body; intimate details of the wife's body). Through the single detail of the windows it is indicated that the house here shares the imposing character of that of Odysseus, on which he remarks, in disguise, in Book 17 (264–5):

Eumaeus, it is clear that this is the fine house of Odysseus,
for it is easy to distinguish among many.

With the sudden shift to the ancient column, which one takes to be on the horizon, like Cape Sounion (colloquially 'Kávo-Kolónes') as seen from off the Attic coast, there is a pretty clear hint at Odysseus as the archetype of the ballad's Exile: Seferis uses the word 'ancient' (ἀρχαῖος) sparingly, and Odysseus as seaman is familiar from 'Upon a Foreign Verse', to look no further. This shift of vision brings about a rupture in the sequence of marks which we have noted: instead of showing wife and marriage-bed as the Exile's destiny Seferis defeats, in the bleakest possible way, the expectations aroused by the title.

The last four lines, then, have stated what *B* is after; but he is far from attaining it: the situation of the later books of the *Odyssey* has been inverted. And the inversion goes further, as we can see from a comparison of the lines that follow with *Odyssey* 17.269–71:

> I know that many men are having dinner
> there, for fumes are rising and the lyre is sounding
> there, which the gods have made the companion of the feast.

These unseen but clearly perceived revellers are replaced by Seferis with the kneeling men everywhere seen by *B*, and this has implications for the outcome of the poem. The enjoyment of the unjust diners in the *Odyssey*, as the Suitors feast in Odysseus' house, is the prelude to the just outcome: Seferis' alteration of the scene to one of prayer leaves us with the suspicion that there will not be a happy ending here. For all this, *A* continues to reiterate his advice, claiming that *B* has already arrived at his house and will soon be welcomed home. This mention of φίλοι alerts us to the very beginning of the *Odyssey* (1.18–19):

> but not even there [in Ithaca] was he free from struggle,
> even among his φίλοι.

The word means in modern Greek simply 'friend', but in Homeric Greek it is anyone with some connection, like the δικοί σου also referred to by *A*. The point here is that there are those among Odysseus' people who are far from friendly; and once again we may cast our minds back to the hero's arrival in Ithaca and his anxious questions (13.200–2):

> Alas, at the land of what mortals have I arrived?
> Are they violent men and savage and not just,
> or hospitable, with a disposition that respects the gods?

These questions, far from being dismissed from our minds by this point in Seferis' 'Return', have taken root: we are worried at the thought of what welcome *B* will actually receive. The next line, however, the first of the sixth section, reveals that to see *A*'s advice 'simply as a trap' – comparable, then, to the ambush that the Suitors unsuccessfully lay for Telemachus – is to over-simplify.[4] For the voice of his friend *A* – that this is what he calls himself we may deduce from his calling *B* 'friend' – is by this point fading away: *A*, then, may be conniving at the threat to *B*, but he is not himself that threat.

At this turning-point in the poem we leave echoes of the Suitors and the second half of the *Odyssey* and turn to the in many ways analogous relation between Odysseus and his Companions in the first. Like all the physical features that surround him, *A* is shrinking away: he still has enough breath – we are to imagine a stage-direction fading out his voice to inaudibility – to reiterate his false assurances, but he himself is doomed. In this passage we come to understand why Seferis has removed from his 'Return' the recognition of husband and wife that is the keystone of the ballad, and for that matter of the *Odyssey*. For recognition in Seferis' poem has turned out to be, not a reciprocal relation, as it is in the successive recognitions between Odysseus and others in the epic, but a one-sided one. *A*, that is, fails to recognize *B* – to recognize what sort of person he is in order to be possessed by such disquiet about the state of his country – just as the Suitors fail to recognize Odysseus until it is too late. (It must be stressed, however, that *B*, unlike Odysseus, is not the agent but the witness of the doom of the impercipient: Seferis identifies himself with Odysseus in his predicaments, but not in his heroic ability to conquer those predicaments.)

On the other hand, *A*'s charge against *B* that he has allowed nostalgia to prevent the attainment of *nostos* seems a reasonable one; and we might start to feel the attraction of the view that *A* and *B* are two halves of the poet himself, and that the poem is one in which the poet is exercising a creative self-criticism.[5] But we must look first at the final section. The voice of *A* disappears because he has sunk completely: βούλιαξε seems appropriate to a watery grave, fitting the case of the Odyssean Companions. Their foolishness lay in not

[4] *Pace* Maronitis, Σεφέρης, p. 41.

[5] Mario Vitti, Φθορὰ καὶ λόγος, εἰσαγωγὴ στὴν ποίηση τοῦ Γιώργου Σεφέρη (Athens 1978), pp. 132–3.

heeding the consequences that would flow from their actions in a world governed by divine laws: in the same way, *A* here fails to see that it is *B*, like Odysseus – and not *A* himself – who has an eye on the laws that govern the real world. As with the Companions, *A*'s flaw is not so much in outright wickedness as in self-deception: Homer is a good psychologist. When the Companions discuss the possibility of killing the Oxen (*Odyssey* 12.345–51) the terms they employ make their lack of realism clear:

> If we do reach Ithaca, our homeland,
> straightaway we shall make a rich temple to the Sun Hyperion
> and place in it many fine statues;
> but if he is at all angry over his straight-horned bulls
> and wishes to destroy our ship, and the other gods assent,
> then I would rather lose my soul with a single gulp at the wave
> than long crawl over a desert island.

The optimism of the first three lines does not seem to be seriously dented by the grave possibility envisaged in the last four. The sophistry that death by drowning is better than death by starvation is false consolation: the Companions do not face the fact that death is death.

'You will return home having lost all your companions': Athena's words (*Odyssey* 13.340) fit the case of *B*. By denying the reader the expected recognition scene (whether with Eumaeus, Telemachus, Eurycleia, Penelope or Laertes) and turning back to the Companions, 'The Exile's Return' becomes a bleak revision of the Odyssean *nostos*.

II

'The Exile's Return', were it to end with the verse,

> my last friend has sunk

would end with a powerful abruptness characteristic of the Greek ballad tradition. But it gains by having two further stages before its completion. The two lines that follow replace what could have been a cry of despair at the loss of the last Companion with a statement in a spirit of philosophical contemplation: everything in the world suffers a periodic change. If the poem ended here we would see it as a sort of fatalistic response to the threat of imminent world war which is apparent in the date which the poet has chosen to append to the poem – but the poet performs a further twist of the knife without sacrificing the overall economy of diction and structure. Two reasons stand out for not ending the poem with the verse,

> is lowered every so often.

The first is internal, related to the unfolding of the poem. To end its second half here would somehow soften the impact of the way in which the first half developed sinisterly up to the pregnant

> to give you a sweet welcome home.

And in fact the poem's last two lines end its second half as forebodingly as ended the first. The focus narrows to 'here'; the harvest is of a threatening kind: 'cross, harvesting' makes the earlier 'is lowered' look like a euphemism which does not do justice to the cosmic cycle in human terms. What brings about the cycle's fulfilment is not the shrinking of what we value, as we have hitherto suspected, but its being cut down by an outside agency.

The last line makes clear that this agency is not divine, like, say, the harvest prophesied by John the Baptist, but human, brought about by human agency. It is not inevitable, furthermore, but the product of military ambitions. Hence the poem's last word, δρεπανηφόρα ('scythe-bearing'), tacked on as it is to χιλιάδες ἅρματα ('thousands of chariots'). An ἅρμα is usually, but not always, for warlike purposes, and so the epithet is needed to make a point, which it does in a strong and unexpected way: δρεπανηφόρα is very much a loaded word, partly because it brings a 'pointedly mixed idiom' to an ostensibly demotic poem, and partly because it brings with it a disruption of the poem's regular metre: a number of Maniat songs in this metrical form end with a metrical change to seal the poem, but the technique is harnessed by Seferis here to very specific purposes.[6] There are two articulations we can make of the last line,

[6] On the idiom: Maronitis, Σεφέρης, p. 42; on the songs, K. Pasayánnis, Μανιάτικα (Athens 1928), e.g. p. 115; and Seferis' imitation of the style in «Ἄνοιξη Μ. Χ.», Ποιήματα, pp. 173–5.

and both emphasize that sinister epithet. If we read the line as a regular nine-syllable verse expanded by two syllables we will break it

χιλιάδες ἅρματα δρεπανη | φόρα.

The last two syllables in this case contain the information that what we fear is not the Reaper but things which are 'scythe-bearing' – that is, man-made. If, alternatively, we read the line with a strong central caesura dividing it into two verses, the first acatalectic and the second catalectic, the epithet in its entirety is set apart and its decisiveness increased by the catalexis:

χιλιάδες ἅρματα | δρεπανηφόρα.

The poem's second part thus ends as sinisterly as the first and indeed rounds it off with an echo of the garden. But we may go on to ask whether there is not in addition a thread of Homeric allusion like that which runs through the first phrase; a look back at *Mythistorema* 24 may help us here. The prediction of future danger there was couched in Iliadic terms, echoing the violent feelings of Agamemnon which brought 'myriad woes' on the Greeks. 'The Exile's Return' too ends with the thought of war: chariots are of course to be found in the *Iliad*, but not with scythed wheels, which add a note of barbarism. Seferis' presentation is characteristic: the destructive effects of war are added to the misfortunes of the journey home but are left in suspense and the events of war itself are not described. Yet in 1938 war is a real prospect, and we are bound then to reflect on the date of the poem and, accordingly, on its politics. Maronitis sums up the matter thus: 'The progress of the composition reveals the insistence of the host as a pure trap, and the stranger's resistance matures into political protest.'[7] The poet is indeed protesting, obliquely – he worked for the Press Office of the fascistoid Greek government – against the inertia of Greece when faced by the prospect of invasion: ἅρματα [μάχης] can be tanks, even if the poet prefers to mythologize them.

[7] Maronitis, Σεφέρης, p. 41.

III

I argued earlier that 'Upon a Foreign Verse', the first attempt on the part of Seferis to make for modern Greek poetry a distinctive sort of access to Homer by linking Homer and the popular tradition, failed at its crucial point, its *Nekyia*; *Mythistorema* 24, by contrast, did not emphasize folk tradition. In 'The Exile's Return' the two traditions are intertwined in a metrical form with sinister associations (that of the Maniat laments, which often express a thirst for revenge after the violent death of a relative), which offers the opportunity for a form of expression somewhere between the staple 'political verse' and the fragmented *vers libre* of *Mythistorema* – Seferis' only collection entirely in free verse – which sets itself against this tradition. The title of Seferis' 'Return', as much as that of *Mythistorema*, has turned out to be a very successful piece of sleight of hand, drawing attention away from its relation to Homer. But sadder and wiser attitudes to Homer, the folk tradition and the national identity after 1922 came all together. What was written in 1914 about the original ballad of the 'Return' by N. G. Politis makes an illuminating object of comparison with Seferis' version:

> It is very well known that the oldest, and incomparably beautiful, original of the [song] version is the episode in the *Odyssey* of the recognition between Odysseus and Penelope.[8]

Nothing could show more clearly the gulf between Seferis' generation and the pre-1922 age; and the poet was able to explore this predicament through recourse to Homer.

[8] N. G. Politis, Ἐκλογαί, p. 120.

Chapter Fourteen
Spirit and letter in 'The King of Asine'

> We shall often find that not only the best, but the most individual parts of [a poet's] work may be those in which the dead poets, his ancestors, assert their immortality most vigorously. And I do not mean the impressionable period of adolescence, but the period of full maturity. T. S. ELIOT[1]

I

'The King of Asine' is as well known as any poem of Seferis, and it is no coincidence that the volume of translations from his poetry that appeared in England in 1948, and which gave Seferis a reputation outside Greece, took the poem for its title.[2] Here we have what in modern Greek is the poem of allusion *par excellence* – but it is one which requires close attention if we are to understand how, coming as it does at the end of a distinct phase of Greek life and letters (the Second World War put the very existence of Greece in doubt), this poem represents not just the personal maturity of Seferis but the coming of age of the problem which has been the subject of this book.

THE KING OF ASINE

and Asine ILIAD

We looked all round the fort all morning,
starting from the shady side, where the sea
green and without reflection, killed peacock's breast,
received us like time without a gap.
The veins of rock came down from high above,
twisted shoots naked with many tendrils coming alive
at the water's touch, as the eye following them
struggled to escape the tiring rocking,
ever losing strength.

[1] Eliot, *Sacred Wood*, p. 48.
[2] G. Seferis, *The King of Asine* (tr. Bernard Spencer, Nanos Valaoritis and Lawrence Durrell, London 1948).

On the sunny side a long open shore
and the light boring diamond shapes on the great walls.
No living creature, the wild doves fled
and the king of Asine for whom we have been searching two years now
unknown, forgotten by all even by Homer,
only one word in the *Iliad* and that uncertain,
thrown down here like a gold funeral mask.
You touched it, remember its sound? Hollow in the light
like a dry jar in dug earth;
and in the sea the same sound as our oars.
The king of Asine a void beneath the mask,
everywhere with us everywhere with us, beneath a name:
'and Asine... and Asine...'
and his children statues
and his desires birds' flutterings and the wind
in the interstices of his thoughts and his ships
moored in an invisible harbour;
beneath the mask a void.

Behind the big eyes, the curving lips, the curls,
in relief on the golden cover of our existence,
a dark point seen travelling like a fish
in the dawn calm of the deep sea:
a void everywhere with us.
And the bird that took flight last winter
with broken wing,
life's tabernacle,
and the young woman who went off to play
with the dog's-teeth of summer,
and the soul which twittering sought the underworld,
and the country like the great plane-leaf carried along by the flood of sun,
with the ancient monuments and the present affliction.

And the poet lingers looking at the rocks and asks himself,
do they exist then,
among these broken lines the points the projections the hollows and the curves,
do they exist then,

here at the meeting-place of the passing of rain wind and
corruption,
do they exist, the movement of the face, the shape of the
affection
of those who have so strangely dwindled in our lives,
of those who are left as shadows of waves and thoughts with the
boundlessness of the deep sea,
or perhaps no nothing remains but only the weight,
the nostalgia for the weight of a living existing thing,
there where we now wait insubstantial, swaying
like the boughs of the horrible willow piled in the duration of
despair
while the yellow flood slowly brings down reeds uprooted from
the mud,
image of a form which has turned to marble at the decision of an
eternal bitterness.
The poet a void.

Shield-bearing the sun continued to rise in battle,
and from the depths of the cave a startled bat
struck on the light like an arrow on a shield:
'and Asine and Asine...'. Perhaps that might have been the
king of Asine
for whom we have been searching so carefully on this acropolis,
sometimes feeling with our fingers his touch on the rocks.

Asine, summer '38 – Athens Jan. '40.[3]

«῾Ο βασιλιᾶς τῆς ᾽Ασίνης»: the title implies the existence of a known person like Agamemnon (ὁ βασιλιᾶς τῶν ᾽Αχαιῶν) in 'Yannis Keats'; but, as things turn out, the king remains a mere hypothesis – which is all he ever could be on the basis of the passage of the *Iliad* (the Catalogue of Ships, 2.559–60) from which the epigraph is taken:

and those who possessed Argos and walled Tiryns,
and Hermione and Asine that command the deep gulf.

The 'king of Asine' in Homer has no existence beyond this: he is a shadow, a hypothetical subordinate of Diomede. The title of Seferis'

[3] Seferis, «῾Ο βασιλιᾶς τῆς ᾽Ασίνης», Ποιήματα, pp. 185–7.

poem, then, turns out to be not a title to glory but an acknowledgement of the anonymity of one who cannot be named; and the epigraph only rubs the point in by specifying as the source the *Iliad*, through which so many heroes have been remembered. Like the epigraph to 'The Companions in Hades' this one too is taken *verbatim* from the Homeric original, but it is of a very different type and function: in 'The Companions' motto and text reflect against each other, while in 'The King' the epigraph is the grit around which the poetic pearl grows, and the words, as we shall see, eventually come to assume a physical presence in the locale described in the poem.

The poem falls into five sections, which I summarize here for clarity before proceeding with the discussion:

lines 1–9: The physical setting of Asine.

lines 10–26: The problem stated: the fragment of Homeric verse corresponds to an archaeological find in that behind both there is a void. (The poem could end coherently here with the posing of the problem.)

lines 27–39: The poem expanded by reflections on the void as something embracing everything that has happened up to our own generation.

lines 40–54: The reflections of the poet in particular, taking the implication that he too, as much as the unknown Homer, is – *ex officio* – a void.

lines 55–60: An epiphany, deliberately made to be of a different sort from that imagined by Sikelianos in 'Secret Iliad' and so expressed with considerable uncertainty.

II

The poem begins like a tourist's diary entry. But 'The King' is not just drawn from observation of a site: in literary terms, the shadow of Eliot appears to fall over the somewhat foreboding description of 'the shady side'. We may compare these lines from 'The Burial of the Dead' (Seferis had published his translation of *The Waste Land* in 1936):

> What are the roots that clutch, what branches grow
> Out of this stony rubbish? Son of man,
> You cannot say, or guess, for you know only
> A heap of broken images, where the sun beats,
> And the dead tree gives no shelter, the cricket no relief,
> And the dry stone no sound of water.

The poet's visit to Asine, as recounted in the poem, does only produce 'a heap of broken images' rather than any solid result from what Eliot elsewhere calls 'the reassuring science of archaeology', as we shall see.[4]

In the second section the perspective shifts, physically and poetically: we move from Eliot to Sikelianos. The key reference to the latter in 'The King of Asine' is, as we shall see, the gold funeral mask (ἐντάφια χρυσὴ προσωπίδα), like the famous 'mask of Agamemnon'; but allusion to Sikelianos goes beyond this.[5] At this point in Seferis' poem we find a correspondence with the opening of 'Yannis Keats': Στῆς Πύλου τὸν πλατὺ γιαλό, τὸ φωτεινό ('at Pylos' broad, bright shore'). But Seferis has taken a turn towards the light without sharing the sunny optimism of Sikelianos' Telemachy: the light here, like that in 'The Burial of the Dead', is oppressive; and the poem will return to this sinister element later.

This is but one of several manifestations of the way in which the 1922 Disaster erects a barrier between the two poems: it radically alters a poet's perspective on Homeric archaeology. 'Yannis Keats' owes something of its vigour to a sense that, through archaeology, modern Greece was recovering its Homeric birthright. Asine, by contrast, was excavated only after 1922, and it is seen by Seferis as a set of ruins created by time's vicissitudes rather than as an ancient survival which can be conjured back to full life by the poet.[6] The landscape is desolate, with the absence not only of the Homeric persons that Sikelianos imagined but of the wild doves of the present. It is as if Seferis is saying *in situ* what Keats muses of the Grecian urn:

> And, little town, thy streets for evermore
> Will silent be; and not a soul to tell
> Why thou art desolate, can e'er return.

But the Greek poet's search for communication with the king of Asine goes on after the visit, as the poet has chosen to remind us by

[4] Eliot, *Sacred Wood*, p. 47. [5] Savidis, «῾Ο Σικελιανὸς καὶ οἱ ῎Αγγλοι ποιητές», p. 99.
[6] See the note in Seferis, Ποιήματα, p. 329.

the date appended to the poem: the two years' search stressed in the poem itself is thus the time of the poem's gestation.[7]

The king, it is emphasized, is *unknown*: that is, nameless and with nothing known about him; forgotten even by Homer because mentioned only in the Catalogue – and then not as an individual – and never thereafter. This line is of some significance for the preoccupation of this book as a whole, for it is the first mention of Homer in the poetry of Seferis.[8] Until this point the impact of the Asia Minor Disaster, as much as a later poet's reticence, has made the very name of Homer hard to use as somehow implicating the poet with a set of presuppositions which he rejects: only now that a poet has assimilated the change in the Greek world, and found a way of creating by the mention of Homer a sense rather of uncertainty than of ancestral pride, can it find an appropriate place.

'Only one word' about the king in Homer, yes – but why 'uncertain'? The poet appears to have taken advantage of a textual variant for thinking the word doubtful; and perhaps there is a more general hint at the pervasive view that the Catalogue of Ships is alien to the body of the *Iliad*.[9] Hence 'thrown down here' in the following line: the word Ἀσίνην is of little consequence to its source. The second half of this line, beginning 'like...' needs to be separated in the reader's mind – the train of thought would admittedly be clearer with a comma, but the poem as a whole is an example of Seferis' conscious practice of minimal punctuation, and a cumulative enjambement runs through these lines. The comparison is not that a gold mask has been thrown down like the word Ἀσίνην – no gold mask was found at Asine, and if it had been it wouldn't originally have been thrown down like that – but that the word is at once random and all that the hypothetical king has as his mask. The derivation of the mask in the poem is not, of course, the real Asine, but 'Yannis Keats' (στὸν τάφο σου... προσωπίδα... ὁλόχρυση): the blend of a real landscape and poetic reminiscences in 'The King of Asine' becomes increasingly hard to separate.

[7] Keeley, *Modern Greek Poetry*, p. 195.

[8] The only other one, significantly refracted through English, is in the poem «Στὰ περίχωρα τῆς Κερύνειας», Ποιήματα, p. 250.

[9] The edition used by Seferis, that of Bérard (Paris 1924), cites an improbable variant Ἀσίην.

The lines that follow also require some disentangling: is 'it' the mask or the word? Grammatically, it could be either, but there is sense in taking the word – using the verb 'touch' no more boldly than we find it elsewhere in Seferis – as the primary object. The presence of the word, then, invites us to 'touch' it as if it were a newly discovered artefact. (Whether or not the poet really did say Ἀσίνην aloud on his visit, this is the idea.) The feeling that a mask just might have a face behind it induces one to touch it; the feeling that a word, said in what are apparently its natural surroundings, might have its referent in some sense *behind it* tempts the superstitious element in us to say it out aloud – perhaps we will learn something from its transference from page to sound. Here the poet describes the sound of the word in two ways, bringing out the twin meanings of κούφιο, neither of which offers him any encouragement: in air, the hollow sound of an empty vessel; in water, the muffled sound made by oars. The point is that the name has no inspiring resonance – and this provokes the fear that it lacks a bearer.

If the name is a mask, of course, we are tempted to talk as if its owner is behind it, as with Agamemnon in 'Yannis Keats' (who is too famous to need naming). Seferis' reiterations 'everywhere with us' reflect the idea he expresses elsewhere of a 'living presence' of Homer, the presence, not of some 'Homeric spirit', but of Homer's very words.[10] The words Ἀσίνην τε are always with us, part of the European literature that begins with Homer; and which, perhaps appropriately, Seferis, rather than Eliot, feels obliged to take up from Homer; but they alone are with us. By their incantation or repetition like 'abracadabra' nothing can be conjured up.

This concentration – to the point of obsession – on Homer's words is another feature that sets 'The King' apart from 'Yannis Keats'. The implicit poetics of Sikelianos is that spirit has pride of place over letter; and while we do find him exploiting the depth of the Greek language this is not the professed aim of an *œuvre* with the title *Lyric Life*. The rhetorical stance of Sikelianos, whatever the real foundations of his achievement, has been summed up thus:

[10] Seferis, Δοκιμές vol. 2, p. 179.

> Poetry is not language and writing, but the hidden secret of life which is bound up with the natural life; the natural life produces the lyric language that sets free the lyricism of nature.[11]

More exacting is the preoccupation in 'The King of Asine' with the lack of fit between spirit and letter. 'Only one word' is not just a quantification of the randomness of Asine's appearance in Homer but an admission of what Homer's Asine is: a mere word, for all that it belongs to the greatest of poets.

The form of the reflections that follow is doubtless indebted to 'Those are pearls that were his eyes' as embodied by Eliot in *The Waste Land* (lines 48, 125). The king's death is seen as a death by water, a failed *nostos*, rather than as a death in battle at Troy; the mention of ships is appropriate, Asine having been a port. But if the form be owed to Eliot, the content has been adapted, once again, from 'Yannis Keats'. In the first place, the children who were very much alive – Nestor's daughters crying out at the sacrifice – are long dead and only their statues remain. Further, while Keats and Sikelianos were

> δεμένοι μὲ τῶν ἔφηβων, ποὺ πέτονται μὲ τοὺς θεούς,
> φτερουγιαστὴ φιλία

(*'bound in the winged friendship of those youths who fly with the gods'*)

Seferis has turned this hyperbole into something utterly insubstantial:

> κι οἱ πόθοι του φτερουγίσματα πουλιῶν.

The king's πόθοι (desires or Cupids) are now the mere fluttering of birds' wings: only the fluttering is left and the love is gone. Again, while Nestor's mind was full of 'holy judgements', the reflections of the less famous king of Asine are spread far and wide now that his spirit has been released into the air of the universe. Finally, the boat of the Telemachus figure in 'Yannis Keats' has been replaced by

[11] Maronitis, Σεφέρης, pp. 96–7.

Seferis with a familiar metaphor for death: the harbour, the after-life, is inaccessible to the senses so lovingly celebrated in 'Yannis Keats' and returns us to the fact that beneath the mask-word there is but a void.

The poem could end here with the failure to conjure up the king of Asine. Before going on to see how it develops, we must take into account a gross omission from the discussion of this second section: Cavafy. The affinity of the inspiration of 'The King' to that of 'Caesarion' has been noted by G. P. Savidis.[12] Even if Cavafy's quest begins, bookishly, indoors rather than in the open air, it too is prompted, at one remove, by archaeology: the book he is ostensibly reading is a collection of inscriptions. Cavafy, too, attempts to create a person, and a king at that, behind the words that he finds; the difference is that he positively relishes the lack of information available:

> In history only a few lines are to be found about you,
> and so I moulded you the more freely in my mind.

The connection of this with Seferis' very different, doubt-plagued 'only one word' is clear enough: what we need to stress as important for 'The King of Asine' is that Cavafy summons up the spirit of Caesarion not just from history but from words – or, to be precise, from the words that *are* history, in Cavafy's pleasingly purist definition – and above all from the word that ends 'Caesarion': Πολυκαισαρίη.

III

The third section of the poem begins with a description of a mask in contrast to our ignorance of what lies behind it; it continues with an inversion of Schliemann's looking upon the face of Agamemnon. Seferis has made out of the simply descriptive πού σκέπασε in 'Yannis Keats' a σκέπασμα: a mask is now seen, not as revealing the face that was once behind it, but as concealing it. The attempt to look behind the mask is tantalizing but fruitless: we can detect a dark point (σκοτεινό meaning dark or obscure), and even follow it

[12] Savidis, Μιὰ περιδιάβαση (Athens 1962), p. 39.

as we might a fish underwater; but this merely confirms a perpetual presence without yielding anything about it.

The lines that follow continue these reflections, not by further defining the elusive nature of the void, but by specifying in seemingly vague or elliptical terms its contents: that is, the past, whether mythologically or historically understood. The use of the word 'tabernacle' (σκήνωμα) brings with it a New Testament sense of the world's impermanence (2 Ep. Pet. 1.13; Matt. 8.20), but the other elements, given the poem's epigraph, can be connected with Homer. The younger woman is a sort of Helen, who frivolously went off with Paris and who describes herself as a bitch (*Iliad* 6.344, 356): the suggestion of the dog-days is therefore appropriate. Rather more perspicuous is the connection of the 'twittering' soul with the souls of the Suitors at *Odyssey* 24.5–10, τσιρίζοντας echoing τρίζουσαι and τετριγυῖαι.[13] But there is also something of the feeling of the lines most famously used of the death of Hector (*Iliad* 22.362–3):

> and the soul, taking flight from his limbs, went down to Hades
> lamenting its fate, leaving behind its manhood and youth.

The plane-leaf is a reminder of the shape of Greece on the map, and brings with it what is perhaps the weak point in the poem. The word 'ancient' (ἀρχαῖος) is a risky one to use in a poem, for reasons we have observed in discussion of the nineteenth century, and as such it is usually avoided by Seferis, or else, as in 'The Exile's Return', worked in with some tact. In 'The King of Asine' the word is portentous, making its entrance rather too prominently into a carefully built up pattern of apposition, expansion and suggestion.

The discovery of the mask serves merely to conceal the obscurity behind it: this third section of the poem has confronted us with both the inexplicability and the bleakness of human – as exemplified by Greek – affairs. Faced with such reflections, Marcus Aurelius had asked: 'What then can send us on our way? One thing and one alone: philosophy.' As we have seen, the ultimate project of *Mythistorema*, as it crystallizes in its last poem, is to substitute poetry for

[13] See the note in Seferis, Ποιήματα, p. 329.

philosophy in this sentence; in the light of this the reflections of the poet that make up this part of 'The King' are natural.

In the fourth section the poem makes a new beginning, in that it returns us to the original visit to Asine. What was initially described as a visit prolonged by collective curiosity has become the solitary lingering of the poet in particular. The anxieties voiced confirm themselves to be a poet's by their allusiveness to Homer, among other texts. The rocks, to begin with – however faithful they may be as a description of Asine in 1938 – also bear the mark of 'Yannis Keats':

> the stone seats which time
> and the folk had made smooth.

What was there perceived as the reassuring process of time whereby the rock was smoothed by human agency in the orderly conduct of life has been transformed by Seferis here into an illustration of time's ferocity. Rocks that once fulfilled human needs have been roughened into a confusion of shapes, and time is now felt to be corruption.

The central question of this section finally takes shape, after interruptions which create suspense. The 'face' (πρόσωπο) is a clear recollection of the human form summoned up by Cavafy in 'Caesarion'; but the love here is affection (στοργή) rather than the *eros* of 'Caesarion'. Cavafy seeks and captures a human expression behind a single word, Πολυκαισαρίη: in imagining expressions behind an immobile, expressionless mask – which has for the reader temporarily taken on an existence of its own instead of simply being the words Ἀσίνην τε – Seferis indicates that his act of imagination is distinctively a poet's by alluding to Cavafy.

With the mention of 'weight' (βάρος), talk of the burden of the past comes naturally, and we construe 'and Asine' as the words which are Homer's and which weigh on the later poem – but the poet cunningly corrects himself in the following line:

> the nostalgia for the weight of a living existing thing.

It is, to be precise, the *weightlessness* of 'and Asine' as a tiny, insignificant mention in Homer, and its failure to reveal a living existing thing behind it, that is oppressive.

The lines that follow expatiate on the powerlessness and meaninglessness of life, in terms of Greek folk tradition, in which a 'shape' is cast in lead at the birth of a child.[14] But there is also an unobtrusive hint at Homer, in which floods are seen as a sign of divine anger; and we gloss the river-imagery of Seferis' poem with these two passages from the *Iliad* (11.492–5, 16.384–92):

> As when a river in full spate goes down to the plain,
> in winter spate down from the mountains, swollen by the rain of Zeus,
> and it carries down many dry oaks and many pines,
> and it throws much rubbish into the salt sea...

*

> As the whole black earth is swollen with a storm
> on an autumn day when Zeus pours water
> in the greatest abundance, when he is ill-tempered, angry with men
> who in the market-place make crooked judgements by force
> and drive out a case, paying the watch of gods no heed;
> and therefore all the rivers flow in full spate,
> and then many sloping ravines come apart,
> and they flow groaning to the swelling deep salt sea
> at an angle down from the mountains and make nought of the works of men...[15]

In the light of these passages we can attribute connotations to the country's being 'carried along' in the third section, and understand παρασέρνω as 'lead astray'. And the poem thus acquires a loosely political dimension which sets it with 'The Exile's Return'.

[14] Compare Seferis, «Ἡ μορφὴ τῆς μοίρας» and «Φωτιὲς τοῦ Ἁι-Γιάννη», Ποιήματα, pp. 193–4, 109–10; and the note on p. 323.

[15] It is worth noting that by May 1940 Seferis was reading Book 19 of the *Iliad* (Μέρες vol. 3 (Athens 1977), p. 191); it seems likely, in that case, that the above passages were near the surface of his memory.

IV

The fourth section ends yet more bleakly than the third: the poet's reflections seem to have forced on him the conclusion that human (and in particular Greek) affairs are not just transitory but doomed to bitterness. With the impossibility of retrieving anything that we really value, anything really alive, from the past, the very function of the poet seems empty. 'The King''s second section took particular force from the fact that Homer is a void behind the monuments of his poems: the fourth section appears to make every poet a void.

But we saw of the last poem of *Mythistorema* that it found a place for poetry through a plea for a future *Nekyia*, and that this humble and merely envisaged *Nekyia* stood in the starkest contrast with the triumphant epiphany of Achilles in Sikelianos' 'Secret Iliad'; and the same is true here of the still more tentative *Nekyia* which, so to speak, concludes 'The King of Asine'. The sun rising ἀσπιδοφόρος (shield-bearer) hints at Homer – both at ornamental epithets of warriors and at the way in which the rising or falling of the sun can indicate changing fortunes in battle (e.g. *Iliad* 8.68) – and the bat flying up out of the cave connects not just with the sun as shield ('Ασπιδοφόρος with σκουτάρι) but also with the descent of the soul, implicitly compared with a bat, earlier in the poem. But there is also a contrast with 'Secret Iliad'. The fear with which the soul here emerges from the Underworld sets it apart from the bloodthirsty strength of the shade of Achilles as Sikelianos imagines him returning to his rightful place in the defence of Greece; and the contrast is sharpened by the fact that Achilles is a national hero while the king of Asine is an unknown. Achilles returns with a battle-cry; the king of Asine with a bat's squeak, the colon pointing us to 'and Asine and Asine' as being, as it were, the notation of the sound made by the bat. The very same words of Homer now answer the earlier invocation, whose efficacy we had since come to doubt; and they do so with the rapidity of the bat's appearance: the dots are removed from the middle of the repeated quotation.

This, however, is no more than a hesitant adoption of the hope that the king of Asine has said anything to us: a bat's squeaks are inscrutable. (Indeed, my way of pinning down the passage may properly provoke unease for making what is so tenuous and inexplicit cut-and-dried.) But there has arisen at least the possibility of something corresponding to the *Nekyia* of *Mythistorema* 24, a reticent answer, in time of war, to 'Secret Iliad'. As a response to the times this is fitting: the poet asks for hope, but in the face of the certain sufferings of 1940 this is a muted hope indeed compared with the delusions of the Great Idea. And yet with the last line of the poem the hope for something tangible can now, after a fashion, be endorsed. Though the king's touch no longer exists we can settle for 'feeling his touch': there is no longer the certainty that the king is a void. Hence the protracted last two lines: the thought that the bat is the king leads to, but is eclipsed by, the limited contact physically achieved with the place Asine.

I have concentrated here on what I see to be Homeric elements in 'The King of Asine', and I have not set out to explicate everything in this long and challenging poem. I have tried to show, above all, the power of the way in which the preoccupation with Homer's words grows out of, and finally returns us to, a landscape. 'The King of Asine', in a peculiarly Greek way, goes beyond the merely bookish, and in the case of the Greek poems which owe a debt to Homer that is no mean feat.

Reflections

I

Two questions, above all, may be in the mind of the reader who has followed the argument of this book and thought for himself about the constellation of poems discussed. The first: is Homer still a figure of importance for the Greek poets, or has the phase which is the subject of this book come to an end? The second: what, on reflection, is Homer's *distinctive* importance, poetically speaking, for the modern Greek poet? Both questions may briefly be addressed at this point.

Seferis, by 1940, may almost be said to have made Homeric allusion his private property – so much so that the younger Nobel laureate, Elytis, appears deliberately to have drawn less on Homer than on ancient lyric poetry; though we must not discount differences of temperament here.[1] Homeric references, indeed, pervade Seferis' poetry right to the end; and his interest remains centred on the *Nekyia*, which is at the heart of the three important poems, 'Strátis the Seaman Among the Agapanthi' (1944), '*Thrush*' (1947) and 'Memory I' (1955).[2] The first of these poems, written in the Transvaal in 1942, is an urgent adaptation of the *Nekyia* problem to fit the particular circumstances of the poet's diplomatic peregrinations during the War. At this time of despair, the difficulties of communication with the dead are aggravated, first by the voyaging itself, which is understood as running parallel to the episode of Aeolus in the *Odyssey* (10.1–79), and secondly by the alien vegetation of foreign parts: instead of the asphodels that are a familiar part of the Greek landscape and of the Greek Underworld, the poet is faced here with African lilies, agapanthi. The blending of the Wanderings and the *Nekyia* here shows great powers of concentration; the poem is one of the most haunting produced by the War.

[1] See Iakov, Ἡ ἀρχαιογνωσία τοῦ Ὀδυσσέα Ἐλύτη.

[2] Seferis, «Ὁ Στράτης Θαλασσινὸς ἀνάμεσα στοὺς ἀγάπανθους», «Κίχλη», «Μνήμη Α΄», Ποιήματα, pp. 196–7, 217–29, 245–6.

What has proved most influential in the poem, however, is the presence of Elpenor named among the Companions. The youngest of the Companions, we recall, Elpenor fell into a drunken sleep on the roof of Circe's palace and on waking in the morning fell and broke his neck. When Odysseus later arrives in Hades, he is met by the shade of Elpenor who pleads with him to bury his body on the shore with his oar (*Odyssey* 10.552–60, 11.51–78). The theme appeared earlier in the poem from *Mythistorema*, 'Argonauts'; but the distinctive importance of Elpenor in 'Stratis the Seaman', and still more in '*Thrush*', derives, I suggest, from his presence in Pound's Canto I, which Seferis translated in 1939. The poet of the *Odyssey* seems to have introduced Elpenor in an effort to humanize the mythical descent of Odysseus to Hades; to subordinate this magical part of the story to the poem's overriding preoccupation with the human problem of Odysseus' return. But Pound's resonant mistranslation of the line

> ἀνδρὸς δυστήνοιο, καὶ ἐσσομένοισι πυθέσθαι
>
> (11.76: '[*and build me a burial mound on the shore of the grey sea*], *a wretched man's, so that future men may know of it*')

as 'A man of no fortune, and with a name to come' promotes Elpenor to the very centre of the poet's concern with an after-life among men, and it is in this vein that Elpenor takes on a greater importance for Seferis. Seferis' juniors, furthermore, have found Elpenor to be an illuminating case for their attention as political poets: I am thinking here primarily of Yánnis Rítsos (b. 1909) and Tákis Sinópulos (1917–81).[3] Contemporary Greek poetry alludes to Homer sufficiently often as to suggest that this legacy of Seferis persists; but the question can fairly be raised whether the poets after Seferis have drawn so deeply, widely and independently from the Homeric poems as to be able to transcend the Seferian outlook rather than simply respond to it. It is worth glancing here at two palpably post-Seferian poems.

The first is by Ritsos, the Lenin Prizewinner, and was published in 1966:

[3] See Savidis, Μεταμορφώσεις τοῦ Ἐλπήνορα (Ἀπὸ τὸν Πάουντ στὸν Σινόπουλο) (Athens 1981).

NON-HERO

He who, hearing his comrades' tread
going away on the pebbles, in his drunkenness,
instead of coming down the ladder he had climbed up, jumped
straight down,
breaking his neck, arrived first
at the black opening. And he had no need
of those prophecies of Tiresias. And he did not even touch
the black ram's blood. The one thing he asked for
was a yard of ground on the shore of Aeaea
and for them to set his oar there – the one with which he used
to row
next to his comrades. Honour, then, and glory
to the handsome lad. They said he was light in the head. And yet
didn't he too help to the best of his ability
in their great journey? It is for this, indeed, that the Poet
picks him out for special mention, albeit with a certain superiority,
but perhaps for that very reason with the more love.[4]

A first reading might take this as a very crude rebuttal of the Seferian Elpenor: Seferis, taking on the guise of the 'real' hero, Odysseus, needs the black blood of inspiration and appropriates it to himself; Ritsos' Elpenor, by contrast, is proud, not of his distinctiveness, but of his role in a collective effort. But the virtue of Ritsos' poem is that, while rejecting Seferis' lone Odysseus, it also looks positively to something that is there in the *Odyssey*: the human presence of Elpenor as a figure eliciting our sympathy. The poem, indeed, draws on Cavafy's 'Caesarion', and perhaps could not have taken this turn without it: it is precisely those who have not left their mark who are those most prized by the poet.

A more discursive and complex post-Seferian poem alluding to Homer has been written by Pános Thasítis (b. 1925). It is entitled σπιλάδες τε πάγοι τε, which looks like 'squalls and icebergs' but which in the Homeric Greek of the poem's epigraph (*Odyssey* 5.404–5) means 'sharp rocks and reefs':

For there were no harbours which hold ships, nor beaches to
pull ships up on,
but there were projecting coasts and sharp rocks and reefs.

[4] Yánnis Rítsos, Μαρτυρίες Β′ (Athens 1966), p. 103.

The reference is to perhaps the most lonely and perilous moment for Odysseus: having left Calypso, the hero sets off home, but becomes the victim of the anger of Poseidon: only the magic veil given him by the nymph Leucothea saves him from a watery grave. Thasitis' poem is quite a long one (57 lines) and I shall cite here just its core, which picks up the Homeric reference in the epigraph. The poem as a whole is a view of the Aegean, not as a place of beauty and consolation (as in the poetry of Elytis), but as an unyielding and threatening thing, as it can indeed be in stormy weather.

> Wide and easy the road through the gardens,
> beneath the pomegranate-trees' castanets,
> by July's fruit-trees.
> From the one water to the other large pansies of the shadows,
> drugged fig-trees, hiders of desire.
> Like this, leaving the terrible scythe of noon.
> Higher up, it narrows. Paved it ascends,
> stubbornly turns along the hard burnt hills,
> takes to the mountain alone,
> spreads tight branches towards the country chapels,
> abandoned saints, poor votive offerings to the purple Almighty,
> – bodies that were in pain and ended in pain –
> the dry stone ruined for so many years,
> flowers all round upright like lances,
> the hedge sent by heaven and punished by earth,
> rocks, fired whetstones of the sun
> and all the caves from the sea side impassable,
> treasuring up the gigantic roar of the sea,
> the voice of Disseas who was saved with the veil of Leucothea
> beneath his breast,
> deaf to the lost crews of the 'Maid of the Annunciation'
> of the 'Defiant', of the 'Bália',
> to the lament of the women beneath the black cloth
> which suddenly stretched,
> separating sun from whitewash.[5]

In this central section, with the following of the road from the sea we follow with it a train of thought. At first there is a consoling

[5] Pános Thasítis, Ἑκατόνησος (Athens 1971), pp. 16–17.

refuge from the harshness of the elements, but we then emerge into a more rugged landscape higher up, where ruined chapels provoke melancholy thoughts about human pain and failure. The rocks on the heights return the poet's thoughts to the rocks of the sea, to the caves: while Odysseus was saved by divine intervention so many ordinary mortals have been allowed to be lost. The citation of the passage from the *Odyssey*, somewhat elliptically, in the original, is not mere pedantry, I think: it serves to validate the point that the deliverance of Odysseus remains part of the collective memory as the loss of the ships is not. The contrast between the Homeric hero and modern men brings out sharply the sense of the poem that the Aegean is a deadly place. It is not fanciful, perhaps, to stress the fact that this poem was published in 1971, under the seven-year dictatorship, and the poet, in travelling from his adopted home, Thessaloniki, to his native island of Lesbos, would have to pass by the prison island of Áyios Efstrátios. The Homeric poems remain a recourse for those who wish to speak of the present.

II

'No doubt it is advantageous for a Greek poet to employ ancient myths, because he thus becomes more accessible to foreign readers.'[6] Elytis clearly has a point here; and the sceptic might go on to suggest that there has been nothing in this study to show that the difference between the modern Greek poet's relation to Homer and any Western poet's relation to Homer is one of kind rather than degree. It might even be alleged that all Homeric allusion in modern Greek poetry was in the nature of a public-relations exercise: that it cashes in on an inclination to believe, with Joyce (who knew a little ancient, and rather more modern, Greek), that 'the best gate of entry to the spirit of ancient Greece is the modern Greek'.[7] More generally, we might as readers of poetry be attracted by Philip Larkin's anarchism:

> As a guiding principle I believe that every poem must be its own freshly created universe, and therefore have no belief in

[6] Elytis in Keeley, *Modern Greek Poetry*, p. 139.

[7] Frank Budgen, *James Joyce and the Making of 'Ulysses'* (London 1972), p. 174; see also Richard Ellmann, *James Joyce* (2nd edition, London 1982), p. 408.

> 'tradition' or a common myth-kitty or casual allusions in poems to other poems or poets, which last I find unpleasantly like the talk of literary understrappers letting you see they know the right people.[8]

But the present study has attempted to show no more than that there are distinguished poems in modern Greek in which Homer, in some way or other, is a shaping presence. This does not oblige us to believe that Homer is central to the modern poetry as a whole. Indeed, one could remove Homeric allusion from the poetry of modern Greece – not just *verbatim* allusion, that is, but the very existence of Homer – and be left with a poetry of much the same distinction. Nearly all of Cavafy's best work would be left; most of the best poems of Sikelianos; and perhaps the very best of Seferis – to make no mention of others. The aspiration to assimilate Homer, then, is not present in every Greek poet – but few are wholly exempt from it: Kariotakis is perhaps the only poet of distinction in whose work (apart from the collection title *Nepenthe*, of which Baudelaire is the proximate source) there is no trace of Homer. A critical preoccupation with Homer is not necessarily a falling for national myths, a belief that Homer, at any rate, ought to be important to the modern Greek poets. For Homer, as we have seen, does constitute a focus for the aspirations of the modern Greek poets – sometimes conflicting aspirations – and this is not the least of the considerations which make it possible to speak of a coherence in modern Greek poetry as we can speak of few other coherent things in the national life. The verbal interrelations between the relevant poems of Cavafy, Sikelianos and Seferis in particular are one sign of a pattern independent of the imposition of any arbitrary or self-fulfilling notion of Greekness. Even if the myth of the Shade of Homer was in itself poetically unprofitable, Homer, exerting an influence often in an unobtrusive and unexpected way, can be seen as a heavenly body shining over later Greek poetry from which the moderns borrow light.

Ultimately the case for the modern Greek poets as poetic heirs of

[8] Philip Larkin, *Required Writing* (London 1983), p. 79.

Homer must rest on their use of the same language, however altered. Hardy wrote, in a poem on Liddell and Scott's Greek Lexicon, of

> Words, accents not to be breathed by men
> Of any country ever again

and in fact went on to cite the Homeric word ἀάατον, the very first in the lexicon after alpha.[9] But it had not occurred to Hardy to think of the Greek poets of his time and of their efforts to breathe life into, and to derive inspiration from, the words of their ancestors. For, while the modern Greek poet does not of course have the option of writing seriously in Homeric Greek he is still able to exploit expressively a linguistic continuity *or discontinuity* between Homer's language and his own. This is not, to be sure, the key to a poem's success if it happens to allude to Homer, nor is it the key to unlocking any given poem's success; but it is one way, and a neglected way, into this sort of poem; and it is one that this book has attempted to explore. The existence of different registers of Greek within these poems can be telling: in Cavafy's Τὰ ἄλογα τοῦ Ἀχιλλέως we have a tension between the Homeric scene and the modern word for a horse; Sikelianos' subtitle to 'Achelous', ΟΝΕΙΡΟΣ, brings the reader into the past of an actual river normally known as the Aspropotamos, and beyond that to the element Water; Seferis rehabilitates the word ἔρεβος, peeling away metaphor. In all three cases we find what Eliot calls 'the contact which makes it possible for the modern language perpetually to draw sustenance from the dead'.[10]

Though Greek poets are well advised to be sparing with the resources at their disposal, the upshot is clear: while it is neither a necessary nor a sufficient condition for the success of any poet in alluding to Homer, it is the unity of the Greek language which presents him with peculiar opportunities and challenges. In English poetry any allusion to Greek risks being feebly recondite or palpably incongruous, and perhaps the only poet to make it a memorable device was Pound, in *Hugh Selwyn Mauberley*. The most famous

9 Thomas Hardy, *Collected Poems* (London 1952), pp. 805–6.
10 Eliot, 'Classics in English', *Poetry* 9 (November 1916), 101–4.

example plays deliberately on a linguistic coincidence in order to rail against a lack of cultural coherence:

> O bright Apollo,
> τίν' ἄνδρα, τίν' ἥρωα, τίνα θεόν
> What god, man or hero
> Shall I place a tin wreath upon?

This is a virtuoso effect, indeed, but twentieth-century Greek has in this area a greater variety of effects on which to draw; and while it is usually the critic, if it is anyone, who stops to investigate them, the *continuities* of Greek, as we may call them, are often, not always consciously, felt even by an auditor.[11] Homer's words, still present in the language, continue to exert their power; and it is possible for the Greek poet, in ways perhaps not imagined by Eliot, to write with a sense that 'the whole of the literature of Europe from Homer ... composes a simultaneous order'.[12]

[11] Bernard Knox, 'Oedipus Rex', *Grand Street* 4.2 (1985), 203–15.

[12] Eliot, *Sacred Wood*, p. 49.

FURTHER READING

The following is a very selective list of books which may be helpful to the reader who wishes to place the subject of this book in a wider context or to obtain further basic information about matters discussed in it.

1. *History and culture*

Richard Clogg, *A History of Modern Greece* (2nd edition, Cambridge 1986)
John Campbell and Philip Sherrard, *Modern Greece* (London 1968)
A. J. Toynbee, *The Greeks and Their Heritages* (Oxford 1981)
Speros J. Vryonis, Jr (ed.), *The 'Past' in Medieval and Modern Greek Culture* (Los Angeles 1978)
Michael Herzfeld, *Ours Once More: Folklore, Ideology and the Making of Modern Greece* (Austin 1982)

2. *Language*

Peter Mackridge, *The Modern Greek Language* (Oxford 1985)
Robert Browning, *Medieval and Modern Greek* (2nd edition, Cambridge 1983)
Peter Bien, *Kazantzakis and the Linguistic Revolution in Greek Literature* (Princeton 1977)

3. *Literature, general*

C. A. Trypanis, *Greek Poetry from Homer to Seferis* (London 1981)
Linos Politis, *A History of Modern Greek Literature* (tr. Robert Liddell, Oxford 1973)
K.Th. Dimaras, *A History of Modern Greek Literature* (tr. Mary P. Gianos, London 1974)
Philip Sherrard, *The Marble Threshing Floor* (London 1956) and *The Wound of Greece* (London 1978)
Zissimos Lorenzatos, *The Lost Center* (tr. Kay Cicelli, Princeton 1980)
Edmund Keeley, *Modern Greek Poetry, Voice and Myth* (Princeton 1983)

4. *Literature, major poets*

Romilly Jenkins, *Dionysius Solomós* (Cambridge 1940)
Kostis Palamas, *The Twelve Lays of the Gipsy* (tr. George Thomson, London 1969)
Robin Fletcher, *Kostes Palamas. A Great Modern Greek Poet* (Athens 1984)

C. P. Cavafy, *Collected Poems* (with a translation by Edmund Keeley and Philip Sherrard, Princeton 1975)

Robert Liddell, *Cavafy. A Critical Biography* (London 1977)

George Seferis, *Collected Poems* (with a translation by Edmund Keeley and Philip Sherrard, London 1982); *On the Greek Style* (tr. Rex Warner and Th. D. Frangopoulos, London 1966); *A Poet's Journal* (tr. Athan Anagnostopoulos, Cambridge, Mass. 1974)

5. *Homer*

Any bibliography for the Homeric poems is clearly out of place here, but a book which deserves mention as stimulating thoughts about the relation of Homer to the modern Greeks is J. Th. Kakridis, *Homer Revisited* (Lund 1971).

REFERENCES

This list does not include items listed under Further Reading.

Adkins, A. W. H. *Poetic Craft in the Early Greek Elegists* (Chicago 1985)
Aleksándru, Áris. Ποιήματα (1941–1971) (Athens 1972)
Angelomátis, Hrístos E. Ἑλληνικὰ ρωμαντικὰ χρόνια (Athens n.d.)
Arnold, Matthew. *Essays Literary and Critical* (London 1907)
Bate, Jonathan. *Shakespeare and the English Romantic Imagination* (Oxford 1986)
Bate, Walter Jackson. *The Burden of the Past and the English Poet* (London 1970)
Beaton, Roderick. *Folk Poetry of Modern Greece* (Cambridge 1980)
'Myth and Text: Readings in the Modern Greek Novel', *Byzantine and Modern Greek Studies* 9 (1984–5), 29–53
Bloom, Harold. *The Anxiety of Influence* (New York 1973)
A Map of Misreading (New York 1975)
Brower, Reuben A. *Alexander Pope: the Poetry of Allusion* (Oxford 1959)
The Poetry of Robert Frost: Constellations of Intention (Oxford 1963)
Budgen, Frank. *James Joyce and the Making of 'Ulysses'* (London 1972)
Bush, Ronald. *The Genesis of Ezra Pound's Cantos* (Princeton 1976)
Cambon, Glauco. *Ugo Foscolo, Poet of Exile* (Princeton 1980)
Campbell, D. A. (ed.). *Greek Lyric Poetry* (London 1967)
Cavafy, C. P. [K. P. Kaváfis]. Ἀνέκδοτα ποιήματα (1882–1923) (ed. G. P. Savidis, Athens 1968)
'Ars Poetica' (ed. A. Decavalles), *The Charioteer* 10 (1968), 69–80
«Τὸ τέλος τοῦ Ὀδυσσέως» (ed. G. P. Savidis), Δοκιμασία 2 (1974), 9–22
Ποιήματα (2 vols., ed. G. P. Savidis, Athens 1981)
Τὰ ἀποκηρυγμένα. Ποιήματα καὶ μεταφράσεις (1886–1896) (ed. G. P. Savidis, Athens 1983)
Ἀνέκδοτα σημειώματα ποιητικῆς καὶ ἠθικῆς (ed. G. P. Savidis, Athens 1983)
Dállas, Yánnis. Ἐποπτεῖες Α′ (Athens 1954)
Καβάφης καὶ ἱστορία (Athens 1974)
Daskalópulos, Dimítris. Ἐργογραφία τοῦ Σεφέρη (Athens 1979)
Dawkins, R. M. [review]. *Journal of Hellenic Studies* 54 (1934), 106–7
De Quincey, Thomas. *Works* (Edinburgh 1890), vol. 6
De Quincey as Critic (ed. John E. Jordan, London 1973)
Dimarás, K. Th. Νεοελληνικὸς διαφωτισμός (Athens 1977)
Ἑλληνικὸς ρωμαντισμός (Athens 1982)
Ἱστορία τῆς νεοελληνικῆς λογοτεχνίας (Athens 1985)

Dodds, E. R. (ed.). *Euripides, Bacchae* (2nd edn, Oxford 1960)
Dragúmis, Íon. Ὅσοι ζωντανοί (Athens 1911)
Dryden, John. *Poems* (ed. James Kinsley, Oxford 1970)
Eliot, T. S. 'Classics in English', *Poetry* 9 (November 1916), 101–4
'Observations', *The Egoist* 5 (1918), 69–70
'The Method of Mr Pound', *The Athenaeum* 24 October 1919, 1065–6
Selected Prose (ed. Frank Kermode, New York 1975)
The Sacred Wood (London 1977)
On Poetry and Poets (London 1979)
Ellis, Steve. *Dante and English Poetry. Shelley to T. S. Eliot* (Cambridge 1983)
Ellmann, Richard. *James Joyce* (2nd edn, London 1982)
Elytis, Odysseas. Τὸ Ἄξιον Ἐστί (Athens 1973)
Erbse, H. (ed.). *Scholia Graeca in Homeri Iliadem* (7 vols., Berlin 1969–88)
Fauriel, Claude. *Chants populaires de la Grèce moderne*, vol. 1 (Paris 1824)
Foscolo, Ugo. *Esperimenti di traduzione dell' Iliade* (3 vols., ed. G. Barbarisi, Florence 1961–7)
Gibbon, Edward. *The Decline and Fall of the Roman Empire* (London 1954), vol. 2
Gifford, Henry. *Poetry in a Divided World* (Cambridge 1986)
Golding, Arthur. *Shakespeare's Ovid, being Arthur Golding's Translation of the Metamorphoses* (ed. W. H. D. Rouse, London 1961)
Haas, Diana. 'Cavafy's Reading Notes on Gibbon's *Decline and Fall*', *Folia Neohellenica* 4 (1982), 25–96
'Early Cavafy and the European "Esoteric Movement"', *Journal of Modern Greek Studies* 2 (1984), 209–44
Hantserís, K. A. Ἑλληνικὸς Νέος Παρνασσός (Athens 1841)
Hardy, Thomas. *Collected Poems* (London 1952)
Harvey, A. E. 'Homeric Epithets in Greek Lyric Poetry', *Classical Quarterly* (n.s.) 7 (1957), 206–23
Hulme, T. E. *Speculations* (ed. Herbert Read, London 1960)
Iakóv, D. I. Ἡ ἀρχαιογνωσία τοῦ Ὀδυσσέα Ἐλύτη (Athens 1982)
Jarrell, Randall. *Kipling, Auden and Company* (New York 1980)
Jenkyns, Richard. *The Victorians and Ancient Greece* (Oxford 1980)
Kakridis, J. Th. 'The Ancient Greeks and the Greeks of the War of Independence', *Balkan Studies* 4 (1963), 251–64
Kálvos, Andréas. Ὠδαί (ed. F. M. Pontani, Athens 1970)
Kariotákis, K. G. Ποιήματα καὶ πεζά (ed. G. P. Savidis, Athens 1972)
Kasínis, K. G. Ἡ ἑλληνικὴ λογοτεχνικὴ παράδοση στὴ «Φλογέρα τοῦ Βασιλιᾶ» (Athens 1980)
Kazantzakis, Nikos. Ὀδυσσέας (Athens 1928)
Ὀδύσεια (Athens 1938)

Keats, John. *Poems* (Oxford 1972)
A Concordance to the Poems of John Keats (ed. M. G. Becker *et al.*, New York and London 1981)
Knox, Bernard. 'Oedipus Rex', *Grand Street* 4.2 (1985), 203–15
Kóndoglu, Fótis. Ἔργα vol. 1 (Athens 1962)
[Koraïs, Adamándios.] Πολιτικὰ φυλλάδια τοῦ Ἀδαμαντίου Κοραῆ (facsimiles, Athens 1983)
Ksenópulos, Grigóris. «Ἕνας ποιητής» (1903), repr. in Ἅπαντα vol. 11 (Athens 1972), pp. 51–60
Ksídis, Theódoros. Ἄγγελος Σικελιανός (Athens 1973)
Larkin, Philip. *Required Writing* (London 1983)
Laskarátos, Andréas. Ποιήματα (ed. E. Moschonás, Athens 1981)
Lavagnini, Renata. 'Le varianti di *Cesarione*', in *Lirica Greca da Archiloco a Elitis. Studi in onore di Filippo Maria Pontani* (Padua 1984), pp. 359–76
Lehonítis, G. Καβαφικὰ αὐτοσχόλια (Athens 1977)
McDougal, Stuart Y. (ed.). *Dante Among the Moderns* (Chapel Hill and London 1985)
Macleod, Colin. 'Homer on Poetry and the Poetry of Homer', *Collected Essays* (Oxford 1983), pp. 1–15
MacNeice, Louis. *Collected Poems* (London 1979)
Markorás, Yerásimos. Ἅπαντα (Athens n.d.)
Maronítis, D. N. Ἀναζήτηση καὶ νόστος τοῦ Ὀδυσσέα (Athens 1982)
«Ὁ μυθολογικὸς Καβάφης καὶ ἡ 'Πριάμου Νυκτοπορία'», Χάρτης nos. 5–6 (1983), 620–9
«Τὰ Καβαφικὰ 'Ἄλογα τοῦ Ἀχιλλέως'», Χάρτης no. 9 (1983), 361–77
Ἡ ποίηση τοῦ Γιώργου Σεφέρη (Athens 1984)
«Κ. Π. Καβάφης: ἕνας ποιητὴς ἀναγνώστης», in Κύκλος Καβάφη (Βιβλιοθήκη Γενικῆς Παιδείας, Athens 1984), pp. 53–80
«Ὁ ἡρωικὸς μῦθος καὶ ἡ λυρικὴ ἀνασκευή του», Διαβάζω no. 107 (1984), 20–6
Mátesis, Andónios. «Ὁ Σολωμὸς καὶ ἡ Ζάκυνθος» in Διαλέξεις περὶ Ἑλλήνων ποιητῶν τοῦ ΙΘ' αἰῶνος ('Parnassus' Society), vol. 1 (Athens 1925), pp. 169–213
Meredith, George. *Poems* (London 1912)
Milióris, N. E. Ἀπόηχοι τοῦ μικρασιατικοῦ ὀλέθρου στὴν ποίηση (Athens 1980)
Mistriótis, G. Κρίσις τοῦ Βουτσιναίου Ποιητικοῦ Ἀγῶνος τοῦ ἔτους 1871 (Athens 1871)
Nietzsche, Friedrich. 'Notes for "We Philologists"' (tr. William Arrowsmith), *Arion* (n.s.) 1 (1973), 279–380
Nikolareïzis, D. «Ἡ παρουσία τοῦ Ὁμήρου στὴ νέα ἑλληνικὴ ποίηση», Νέα Ἑστία no. 491 (Christmas 1947), 153–64

O'Neill, Tom. *Of Virgin Muses and of Love. A Study of Foscolo's Dei Sepolcri* (Dublin 1981)
Orfanídis, Theódoros. Ἅπαντα (Athens 1915)
Padel, Ruth. 'Homer's Reader: a Reading of George Seferis', *Proceedings of the Cambridge Philological Society* 211 (n.s. 31) (1985), 74–132
Palamás, Kostís. Ἅπαντα (16 vols., Athens n.d.)
Ἅπαντα vol. 17: Εὑρετήρια (ed. G. P. Savidis and G. Kehayóglu, Athens 1984)
Pállis, Aléksandros. Ἡ Ἰλιάδα μεταφρασμένη (Paris 1904)
Μπρουσός (ed. E. Moschonás, Athens 1975)
Panayotópulos, I. M. Τὰ πρόσωπα καὶ κείμενα vol. 4 (Athens 1982)
[Paparrigópulos, D.–Vasiliádis, S.], Δ. Παπαρρηγόπουλος–Σ. Βασιλειάδης (Βασικὴ Βιβλιοθήκη) (Athens 1954)
Pasayánnis, K. Μανιάτικα (Athens 1928)
Passow, A. *de comparationibus homericis* (Berlin 1852)
(ed.). Τραγούδια ρωμαίικα – *Carmina Popularia Graeciae Recentioris* (Leipzig 1860)
Pater, Walter. *Marius the Epicurean* (London 1924)
Appreciations (London 1924)
Perídis, Mihális. Ὁ βίος καὶ τὸ ἔργο τοῦ Κωνσταντίνου Καβάφη (Athens 1948)
Polilás, Iákovos. (tr.). Ἡ Ὀδύσσεια (Athens 1875–81)
Polítis, Kosmás. Στοῦ Χατζηφράγκου (Athens 1963)
Eroica (ed. Peter Mackridge, Athens 1982)
Polítis, Línos. (ed.). Ποιητικὴ Ἀνθολογία vol. 4 (Athens 1975)
Polítis, N. G. «Γνωστοὶ ποιηταὶ δημοτικῶν ᾀσμάτων», in Λαογραφικὰ σύμμεικτα vol. 1 (Athens 1920), pp. 211–36
Ἐκλογαὶ ἀπὸ τὰ τραγούδια τοῦ ἑλληνικοῦ λαοῦ (Athens 1969)
Νεοελληνικὴ μυθολογία vol. 1 (Athens 1979)
Pope, Alexander. *Poems* (ed. John Butt, London 1961)
The Iliad of Homer (2 vols., ed. Maynard Mack *et al.*, London 1967)
Pound, Ezra. *Selected Letters* (ed. D. D. Paige, London 1971)
Selected Prose 1909–65 (ed. William Cookson, London 1973)
Cantos (London 1975)
Literary Essays (ed. T. S. Eliot, London 1985)
Prevelákis, Pandelís. Ἄγγελος Σικελιανός (Athens 1984)
Quasimodo, Salvatore. *Selected Writings* (tr. Allen Mandelbaum, New York 1960)
Rangavís, A. R. Ἅπαντα τὰ φιλολογικά vol. 2 (Athens 1874)
Ricks, Christopher. 'Allusion: the Poet as Heir', *Studies in the Eighteenth Century* 3 (ed. R. F. Brissenden and J. C. Eade, Canberra 1976), 209–40

Ricks, D. B. 'Homer and Greek Poetry 1888–1940: Cavafy, Sikelianos, Seferis' (Ph.D., London 1986)
Rítsos, Yánnis. Μαρτυρίες Β′ (Athens 1966)
Ποιήματα 1930–1960 vol. 1 (Athens 1972)
Roïdis, E. D. Ἅπαντα vol. 2 (ed. A. Angélou, Athens 1978)
Ruskin, John. *Fors Clavigera* (London 1871–4)
Sesame and Lilies (London 1884)
Russell, D. A. (ed.). *Longinus, On the Sublime* (Oxford 1964)
and Winterbottom, M. *Ancient Literary Criticism* (Oxford 1972)
Sakellários, Yeóryios. Ποιημάτια (Vienna 1917)
Sandys, J. E. *A History of Classical Scholarship* vol. 3 (London 1908)
Savidis, G. P. Οἱ Καβαφικὲς ἐκδόσεις (1891–1932) (Athens 1966)
Πάνω νερά (Athens 1973)
Μεταμορφώσεις τοῦ Ἐλπήνορα. (Ἀπὸ τὸν Πάουντ στὸν Σινόπουλο.) (Athens 1981)
«Ἑπτὰ στάδια ἑνὸς ποιήματος τοῦ Καβάφη ('Ἡ κηδεία τοῦ Σαρπηδόνος') (1892–1924)» in *Lirica Greca da Archiloco a Elitis. Studi in onore di Filippo Maria Pontani* (Padua 1984), pp. 341–57
«Ὁ Σικελιανὸς καὶ οἱ Ἄγγλοι ποιητές», Νέα Ἑστία no. 1307 (Christmas 1984), 92–103
Μικρὰ Καβαφικά Α′ (Athens 1985)
'The Burden of the Past and the Modern Greek Poet', *Grand Street* 4.2 (1985), 164–90
'The Tragic Vision of George Seferis', *Grand Street* 5.2 (1986), 153–74
Seferis, George. Στροφή (Athens 1931)
The King of Asine (tr. Bernard Spencer, Nanos Valaoritis and Lawrence Durrell, London 1948)
Ἀντιγραφές (Athens 1963)
Δοκιμές (2 vols., Athens 1974)
Ἔξι νύχτες στὴν Ἀκρόπολη (Athens 1974)
Μέρες vol. 1 (Athens 1975), vol. 2 (1975), vol. 3 (1977), vol. 5 (1977)
Μεταγραφές (ed. Y. Yatromanolákis, Athens 1980)
Ποιήματα (ed. G. P. Savidis, Athens 1982)
Shipp, G. P. *Modern Greek Evidence for the Ancient Greek Vocabulary* (Sydney 1979)
Sikelianós, Ángelos. «Γιάννης Κῆτς», Ἀγγλοελληνικὴ Ἐπιθεώρηση 2 (1947), 345–50
Λυρικὸς βίος (6 vols., ed. G. P. Savidis, Athens 1965–9)
Πεζὸς λόγος vols. 1–4 (ed. G. P. Savidis, Athens 1978–84)
Sikutrís, Ioánnis. «Ἐπιλεγόμενα εἰς τὸ ἔργον τοῦ Th. Zielinski Ἡμεῖς καὶ οἱ ἀρχαῖοι» in Μελέται καὶ ἄρθρα (Athens 1956), pp. 93–119

Solomós, Dionísios. Αὐτόγραφα ἔργα (ed. Línos Polítis, Thessaloniki 1964)
"Απαντα (ed. Línos Polítis, Athens: vol. 1 1979, vol. 2 1968)
Tennyson, Alfred Lord. *Poems* (ed. Christopher Ricks, 2nd edn, London 1986)
Thasítis, Pános. Ἑκατόνησος (Athens 1971)
Theotokás, Yórgos. Ἐλεύθερο πνεῦμα (ed. K. Th. Dimarás, Athens 1973)
and Seferis, George. Ἀλληλογραφία (1930–1966) (ed. G. P. Savidis, Athens 1975)
Tomadákis, N. B. «Ὁ Σολωμὸς καὶ οἱ ἀρχαῖοι» in Νεοελληνικά. Δοκίμια καὶ μελέται Β′ (Athens 1983), pp. 7–32
Tsírkas, Stratís. Ὁ πολιτικὸς Καβάφης (Athens 1971)
Turner, Frank M. *The Greek Heritage in Victorian Britain* (New Haven 1981)
Valaorítis, Aristotélis. Ἀριστοτέλης Βαλαωρίτης (2 vols., ed. G. P. Savidis *et al.*, Athens 1980–1)
Vayenás, Násos. Ὁ ποιητὴς καὶ ὁ χορευτής. Μιὰ ἐξέταση τῆς ποιητικῆς καὶ τῆς ποίησης τοῦ Σεφέρη (Athens 1979)
Vitti, Mario. Φθορὰ καὶ λόγος, εἰσαγωγὴ στὴν ποίηση τοῦ Γιώργου Σεφέρη (Athens 1978)
Whitman, Walt. *The Complete Poems* (ed. Frank Murphy, Harmondsworth 1975)
Wildenstein Gallery. *Theophilos, Kontoglou, Ghika, Tsarouchis: Four Painters of Twentieth-Century Greece* (London 1975)
Yannópulos, Periklís. Ἡ ἑλληνικὴ γραμμή (Athens 1965)
Zóras, G. Ὁ Κάλβος καὶ τὸ ὁμηρικὸν χειρόγραφον τῆς Γενεύης (Athens 1969)

INDEX

(*Bold figures indicate major discussions; figures in square brackets indicate pages where the head-word is alluded to but not named.*)